ALL YO

Relaxation

VIKAS MALKANI

New Dawn

NEW DAWN
An imprint of Sterling Publishers (P) Ltd.
A-59 Okhla Industrial Area, Phase-II,
New Delhi-110020.
Tel: 6313023, 6320118, 6916165, 6916209
Fax: 91-11-6331241 E-mail: ghai@nde.vsnl.net.in
www.sterlingpublishers.com

All you wanted to know about Relaxation

ISBN 81 207 2391 0
Reprint 2003, 2006

Published by Sterling Publishers Pvt. Ltd., New Delhi-110020.
Lasertypeset by Vikas Compographics, New Delhi-110020.
Printed at Sterling Publishers Pvt. Ltd., New Delhi

CONTENTS

Dedicated

To: V and A,

For you — Always!

Introduction

Stress has been with us since the beginning of time. Being a part of our response to any challenge or stimulus, it has proved to be a positive force, aiding our continued survival and providing a dynamic that distinguishes between the active business of living and mere passive existence. By shaping our lifestyle, setting the tempo and determining the rhythm at which we live, stress can generate the impetus necessary to convert thought into action, whether that action is making love, conducting an orchestra, running a race, escaping from fire or flood, or meeting a deadline.

But today, life's challenges are far more complex than they used to be, while life itself is altogether a harsher, less natural process than it used to be. Living in an age of immense and increasingly rapid changes, we are subjected to greater, more insistent and inescapable pressures to adapt, keep up, and compete—in short, to survive—than at any other time. Achieving the right balance between too much and too little stress, has become an integral challenge of life.

In fact, some stress researchers suspect that many of us are becoming addicted to our own increased levels of stress hormones, depending on constant challenge as a self-prescribed antidote to the intolerable prospect of boredom.

Answer to the Stress Problem

It is common to all sufferers from stress, whether the over-stress of the fast track or the under-stress of boredom and frustration, to have a feeling of not being in control of their lives. If we think of the people we know who can handle significant amounts of stress and avoid its damaging effects, we will find that they maintain a strong sense of commitment to their work and other activities and respond positively to challenges rather than feeling overwhelmed by them. They seem to be able to recognize the insidious action of repetitive over-arousal before it affects their well-being. They also realize that there is no single solution to the problem of stress – after all, what is stressful for one person is not necessarily stressful for everyone. So the ultimate responsibility for our well-being rests first and foremost with ourselves.

In order to feel in control, we must develop a healthy, stress-proofed lifestyle. Over the past few years, growing awareness of the importance of balanced nutrition, the need for exercise, the dangers of smoking, alcohol and drugs, and the hazards of environmental pollution and ecological imbalance, have fostered a renewed interest in holistic well-being.

We cannot separate our physical health from the well-being of our minds. Both are closely interdependent. In turn, equilibrium of both mind and body is determined largely by the way we communicate and relate to other individuals, and by the symbiotic relationship between society and the environment. Stress can arise in any area of life when we fail to respect the interdependence of human beings and all other living organisms, or if we upset the rhythmic balance of rest and movement, and the complementary cycles of physical and mental activity, of work and leisure activities.

Adapting Your Lifestyle

You can apply techniques of stress management to every area of your life.

At a time when high technology is revolutionizing every aspect of the way we work, it has become more essential than ever to humanize our working environment and our professional relationships and to adopt more flexible attitudes to the structure of employment and our styles of working.

Well-organized people suffer few pressures, scheduling their activities efficiently to minimize the tyranny of time stress.

Most of the lifestyle changes outlined in the book are simple to implement – and you will probably find that you do some of them naturally anyway. But the majority of us have at least one aspect of our lifestyle that requires stress-proofing. Effective stress-management may simply mean making adjustments to your diet, such as, reducing the amount of tea or coffee you drink (caffeine has a marked effect on the amount of adrenalin in the blood); or it may be a matter of adopting one of the relaxation techniques such as yoga, meditation, and massage which helps to develop a more positive and confident attitude to life's challenges; alternatively, it may mean riddance of accumulated nervous energy and tension by taking up more vigorous exercise, to give yourself a feeling of release.

Giving Yourself a Break

Allowing ourselves to become chronically overstressed is often a warning sign that we have stopped paying attention to who we really are.

Learning to give yourself a break, in every sense of the word, needs practice, especially when you are the one who is driving yourself the hardest. But the rewards in terms of regaining self-possession, and restoring the feeling that you have control over your life, can prove incalculable. Having the courage to examine long-held beliefs, to challenge and possibly change your attitudes towards yourself, your work and your relationships, may in turn alter your whole relationship to stress. Recognizing that you have a right to make mistakes, to refuse excessive demands, to say "no", to express your needs and feelings openly, to make time for yourself, and to cater for your wants as well as those of others – all these are central to cultivating a healthy, balanced sense of self-altruism, probably the most basic survival skill of all.

The Causes of Stress

Every day we face some sort of challenge. At home, at work, even at play, out-of-the ordinary demands are imposed on our minds and bodies. Stress is the state of arousal with which the body responds to such demands.

Our response to challenge is prompt, speedy and efficient. When we first perceive the challenge, a chain reaction of automatic bodily processes provides an instant surge of energy and strength, effectively preparing us to fight or to flee.

Earlier in our evolutionary history, our ability to make use of this fight or flight response meant the difference between life and death. Even today, it is just as necessary in certain situations, enabling us to cope with extra demands to the best of our ability. The reflexes that prepare the mind and body to run a race, to perform in public, and to meet deadlines, are identical to those that enabled our early ancestors to deal with attacks from wild animals or invading tribes.

While the causes of stress have vastly changed, our primitive response to them remains unaltered. Civilization has created new pressures that test our ability to survive. We cannot deal with the common, everyday stress situations of the modern world through physical exertion. So our body's response to these challenges is often inappropriate. This is not harmful in itself, provided that we can discharge the energy and tension that are generated through the fight or flight response. But often, persistent stress-bearing situations build up. Physical pressure, which if accumulates, can lead to exhaustion and disease. In order to avoid this situation, we must learn either to release the pressure (for example, by exercising), or to turn off the arousal response by adopting a conscious relaxation technique.

The stage at which manageable, positive arousal turns into unhealthy overstress is different for all of us. Our personality, behaviour, and lifestyle – all have important influences on our stress level. Much stress occurs through emotions such as aggression, impatience, anger, anxiety and fear, all of which kindle the body's stress responses.

Eating an unhealthy diet, smoking, drinking and taking drugs can also contribute further to physical strain. Stress may be generated through work, at home, within relationships, as a result of internal emotional conflict, through environment, diet, ill health, and financial insecurity, as well as through major life events – from childbirth to bereavement, marriage to divorce.

Above all, stress is what we perceive it to be. Some people may thrive on a particular situation, while others may find it terrifying and highly stressful. Too little stimulus can be as stressful as too much but stress only becomes harmful when we cannot control our responses to it. Recognizing this fact is the vital first step to reducing the harmful effects of stress in your life.

Stress and Personality

Personality is the most important influence on the way we respond to all events and situations. The values, attitudes, and behaviour patterns that make up our uniqueness as individuals, ultimately make us more or less vulnerable to stress.

The most deep-rooted component of your personality is your value system. This reflects how you rate yourself in relation to others — and how you see the world in general. Learned at a very early age from those closest to you, this self-rating aspect of your personality is likely to be the most rigid and least flexible.

So the origin of much personal stress lies within your perception or concept of yourself.

Low self-esteem can lead to a number of stress-inducing problems: inability to adapt, willingness to place excessively high demands on yourself, and lack of assertiveness. It can also lead to poor self-expression, so that you harbour negative emotions such as anger, fear, aggression and anxiety, rather than giving vent to them.

But you can alter your view of yourself. This depends on your ability to recognize those behaviour patterns and facets of your personality that may be holding you back.

Personality Types

Psychologists have identified two broad personality types, one of which is more prone to stress than the other. *Type A* is the notorious stress-prone personality whose typical behaviour and lifestyle constantly elicit physical arousal. Type A's are impatient, ambitious, competitive, aggressive, and hard-working; they set high goals and demands for themselves and others; and they are particularly prone to stress-inducing anticipatory emotions such as anxiety. *Type B's,* on the other hand, have a reverse profile. They are equable, calm, relaxed, not overtly ambitious, and less at risk from stress and heart disease.

Stress and Lifestyle

Virtually everything in life is potentially stressful to someone. Unavoidable crises face us all, some time or another: divorce, separation, bereavement, examinations, financial struggle and family conflict. But in addition to these events, there are many other potential sources of stress that are dictated by your own particular lifestyle. These can be far less obvious than the major life-crises, but can have a cumulative, pervasive effect.

If you work in a large crowded city, pursue a demanding and competitive job, and have to battle with the noise and discomfort of daily commuting, you face more potential stresses than a happily married person living quietly in a small country village.

The factor that determines how these affect you is how content and satisfied you are with your lifestyle. Stress is more likely to occur if you find yourself caught against your will in a certain way of life, or if you cannot shape and amend your lifestyle to suit your needs.

Life's Key Stress Points

There are certain areas of our lives where stress is likely to be a particular problem. These broad categories are changes in your lifestyle, challenges associated with your performance (especially at work), emotions such as anxiety and fear, boredom, and the grief associated with bereavement or separation. It is worthwhile being aware of these areas, so that you can prepare yourself for crises centering on these problems and emotions.

Stress Points

- **Change**

Inflexible attitudes, adherence to strict values and routines, as well as fear of the unknown, can create undue stress when change challenges you to take risks and be adaptable. The better your health, the easier it will be to cope.

- **Performance**

We often thrive on stress connected with the challenge of physical performance or a test of our skills. This is healthy, provided that you remain confident, and use up the energy and tension generated by extra demands.

- **Anxiety and Fear**

Negative anticipatory emotions may prolong or amplify the arousal caused by actual events. They may also gear you up to confront situations that never occur. Psychological stress can build up and affect physical well-being.

- **Boredom**

Lack of stimulus or interest at work, unemployment, or retirement may create depression, apathy and stress. Doubts as to whether you are needed or valued can lead to a poor self-image and a sense of alienation.

• **Grief**
Bereavement or loss of a partner through divorce or separation can have a deep, prolonged psychological effect. If grief and anguish remain unresolved, suppressed or unrecognized they can trigger mental or physical breakdown.

The Social Readjustment Scale

Health and survival are based on the body's ability to maintain a balance of all the physical and mental processes. This state of equilibrium is called homeostasis. Bodily arousal is an integral part of the body's general adaptation system through which it adjusts to change and tries to restore homeostasis. Too much change in our lives can overtax our adaptive resources causing illness. The Social Readjustment Ratings Scale, devised by the American doctors T.H. Holmes and R.H. Rahe, cites 41 positive and negative life events valued according to the amount of adjustment needed to cope with them.

Using the Holmes-Rahe scale

Scoring over 300 points in one year greatly increases the risk of illness, 150-299 reduces the risk by 30 per cent, while a score of less than 150 involves a slight chance of illness. But illness is not an inevitable result of change. Your personality and your ability to cope largely determine how well you react.

The Holmes – Rahe Scale

Life event	**Lifechangeunits**
Death of spouse	100
Divorce	73
Marital separation	65
Imprisonment	63
Death of close family member	63
Personal injury or illness	53
Marriage	50
Dismissal from work	47
Marital reconciliation	45
Retirement	45
Change in health of family member	44
Pregnancy	40
Sexual difficulties	39
Gain of new family member	39
Business readjustment	39
Change in financial state	38
Change in number of arguments with spouse	35

Major mortgage	32
Foreclosure of mortgage or loan	30
Change in responsibilities at work	29
Son or daughter leaving home	29
Trouble with in-laws	29
Outstanding personal achievement	28
Spouse begins or stops work	26
Begin or end school	26
Change in living conditions	25
Revision of personal habits	24
Trouble with boss	23
Change in work hours or conditions	20
Change in residence	20
Change in schools	20
Change in recreation	19
Change in church activities	19
Change in social activities	18
Minor mortgage or loan	17
Change in sleeping habits	16
Change in number of family reunions	15
Change in eating habits	15
Vacation	13
Christmas	12
Minor violation of the law	11

Signals of Tension

The human body is superbly equipped to deal with stress – but only up to a certain level. If your adaptive resources become overworked and exhausted, your body ceases to function smoothly. Different organs can become stress targets. Symptoms may arise individually or in various combinations. Chronic stomach upsets, headaches, skin rashes, backpain, irregular breathing patterns and sleeplessness are common early indications that we are pushing ourselves too hard. Psychological symptoms tend to creep up on us more slowly and may be less easy to identify. Behaviour is a prime giveaway of tension. Less noticeable to ourselves, it is those who are close to us who may be the first to read these behavioural signals. Erratic, uncharacteristic behaviour and mood-swings often have their origin in tension.

Physical Signals

The body transmits stress through various channels. Unconscious, nervous reflexes lead to overt physical stress signals. The human body registers stress in a number of places, especially on the head and the feet. Many of these are lifetime habits acquired during childhood. But we may be more prone to them under stress. Habitually touching the hair, ear, or nose, grinding the teeth or biting the lips are common signals, as are foot tapping and turning. More serious signals come in the form of physical stress-related illnesses. These vary according to which organ or system is the weakest link in our physiological make-up.

Mood Signals

Stress affects our mood in a variety of ways. Some mood changes take place on the surface, while others are deeper and more pervasive. Irritability and impatience are hyperactive states, relatively superficial manifestations of underlying anxiety and aggression. Restlessness and frustration, if persistent, can be more serious, developing into full-blown hostility or anger. This can often be caused through lack of control or fulfilment at work. Apathy and boredom are *flat* feelings, often associated with low stimulus. They can be just as stressful as more obviously stressed emotions. Most serious are the *down* emotions, such as guilt, shame and the sense of helplessness or hopelessness, as well as depression and fatigue, which are often linked. If longlasting and severe, a downward and negative mood slide indicates more serious, underlying psychological problems.

Behavioural Signals

Any behaviour which indicates that you are not acting your usual self, may be a sign of adverse reaction to stress. Characteristic *type A* behaviour patterns include leaving important tasks undone until the very last minute then panicking and being unable to complete them; allowing insufficient time to get to work and to important appointments, trying to do two or more things at the same time and eating while working.

Stressed behaviour can impair our ability to communicate well. Talking too fast, too loud, or too aggressively, swearing, interrupting others or talking over them, not listening to what people have to say, and arguing for the sake of it, are typical ways in which stress alters our behavioural relationships with other people. Nodding off during meetings or social gatherings, trying to do without sleep, losing one's sense of humour, moving in a tense or jerky way, and reacting nervously or irritably to everyday sounds are other signs.

Outbursts and overreactions can occur when we lose our perspective on problems that we would normally face with equanimity. The occasional outburst, whether of anger or of tears, may be a valid, healthy way to release pent-up tension. But if repeated over a long period, overreactive behaviour may indicate serious problems.

Consistently acting and feeling out-of-character is a serious warning that we are losing our ability to cope with tension. Inability to feel or express any emotion or a sense of being "on automatic pilot", acting more like a robot than a human being, indicates loss of contact with our surroundings and ourselves. Common symptoms include: the inability to make decisions, mind changes, memory blocks, loss of short-term memory, and lapses of concentration. Inhibitions and anxiety when faced with everyday challenges are further symptoms.

Stress Signals

Nervous reflexes

Biting nails, clenching fists, clenching jaw, drumming fingers, grinding teeth, hunching shoulders, picking at facial skin, picking at skin around fingernails, tapping feet, touching hair.

Stress-related illnesses

Asthma, back pain, digestive disorders, headaches, migraines, muscular aches and pains, sexual disorders, skin disorders.

Mood changes

Anxiety, depression, frustration, habitual anger or hostility, helplessness, hopelessness, impatience, irritability, restlessness.

Behaviour

Aggression, disturbed sleep patterns, doing several things at once, emotional outbursts, leaving jobs undone, overreactions, talking too fast or too loud.

Assessing the Stress in Your Life

The questionnaires on the following pages are designed to help you pinpoint the areas of your life where stress is occurring. As you ask yourself each question, bear in mind that there are usually ways of putting a situation right by changing external factors, but that there are also factors within the self that can cause stress. Accumulated stress can sometimes lead to generalized emotions of fear, anxiety, or depression, which are difficult to attribute to any single cause.

Your Environment
Do you never seem to have enough room to put things? Is your home too small and cramped? Do you need more space at home in which to work? Do you feel that you do not have enough privacy? Do you find it difficult to relax at home in the evenings? Are your neighbours too noisy? Do you feel depressed in the dark winter months? Do you wake up in the morning with a stiff back? Do you feel uncomfortable after sitting for a long period?

Yourself
Do you feel trapped in a set of circumstances you cannot change? Do you feel you have many faults and few good points?

Do you feel anxious about talking to strangers?

Do you often suppress your own views because you think other people will be offended?

Do you often give up something you want to do because of what other people want?

Do you find it difficult to talk about your problem?

Do you often put off doing things until the last minute because you are anxious about the difficulties involved?

Do you panic easily when faced with a difficult situation?

Do you spend a lot of time worrying about the future?

Do you lose your temper easily?

Do you burst into tears at the slightest provocation?

Do you feel guilty or depressed when you fail to reach your own targets or goals?

Do you find it difficult to relax?

Do you feel that your talents are very limited?

Do you find it difficult to prepare for the stressful times in your life?

Your Relationships

Do you feel you never have any time for yourself?

Do you argue a lot about money?

Do you feel that you do not have enough privacy at home?

Do you feel guilty that you do not do more for your family?

Do you feel disappointed because your partner cannot live up to your ideal?

Are you finding it difficult to settle down into a permanent relationship?

Do you find it difficult to talk about sex with your partner?

Do you feel that some of your sexual needs or preferences are abnormal?

Do you often feel too tired to make love?

Is there ill-feeling in your family because some members never seem to pull their weight?

Do you find it a problem when children answer back or are rude to you?

Is your family resentful that you do not spend enough time at home?

Are you frustrated because you do not see enough of your friends?

Do you feel resentful because your partner earns more than you?

Your Job

Do you feel put-upon or feel you are working too hard?

Do you regularly work during lunchtimes or evenings?

Do you never have holidays?

Are you depressed by your working environment?

Do you find it difficult to cope with a recent promotion?

Do you feel unable to ask your boss for a rise or a holiday?

Do you feel bored with your job?

Do you find it difficult to organize your work, or are you required to do too many different things at once?

Do you find it difficult to delegate work to someone else when you get busy?

Do you find it difficult to get on with some of your colleagues?

Do you think that communication channels are very poor at your place of work?

Does your job involve the pressure of constant deadlines?

Do you find that constant interruptions ruin your concentration?

Do you work in a very noisy, stuffy or smelly environment?

Do you feel your talents or abilities are not fully recognized?

Do you have to work at relentless, mechanical tasks without the chance to rest?

Your Management of Time

Do you usually try to do things as quickly as possible?

Do you run out of time when working on important projects?

Do you deliberately try to do several things at once?

Do you regularly forget about appointments or important deadlines?

Do you rarely plan any of your activities more than a day or two in advance?

Do you talk and walk quickly?

Do you get impatient easily?

Do you always feel in a hurry?

Do you feel that time is passing by too quickly?

Does time spent on travelling get you down?

Do you always travel to work in the rush hour?

Does your partner often get annoyed because you spend too much time working?

Do you only rarely give yourself a break to play, relax, laze or day-dream?

Do you spend the majority of time with other people, with little time on your own?

Do you feel you spend too much time at home with the children?

Do you often lose your temper because there never seems to be enough time to finish what you need to do?

Do you never use a diary?

Your Diet and Exercise

Do you regularly take less than half an hour for main meals?

Do you often eat while you are doing other things, such as working, travelling, reading, cooking or watching television?

Do you eat a lot of high-calorie foods that produce an instant energy "high"?

Do you regularly eat any of the following: canned foods, refined foods, convenience foods, fatty or fried foods, vegetables that have been stored for long periods?

Do you drink more than five cups of tea or coffee a day?

Do you drink more than 4 glasses of wine, 4 measures of spirits, or 2 pints of beer a day?

Do you regularly have snacks between main meals?

Do you put on weight very easily or quickly?

Do you get a lot of colds or virus infections?

Do you smoke cigarettes?

Do you never set aside some time every day for some form of conscious relaxation?

Do you rarely allow yourself a rest period during the day?

Do your daily activities rarely include some degree of physical exertion (such as walking briskly, chasing young children around, or doing moderate physical work)?

The Art of Being

The way we see ourselves shapes everything we do. Stress is unlikely to be a major problem in your life if you are confident and can control your actions and your destiny.

When life becomes intolerably stressful, the temptation is often to blame external influences. But it is often we, who are responsible for holding ourselves back from getting the most out of life and realizing our full potential.

We can form fulfilling, well-balanced, relationships with others only when we ourselves are fulfilled and well-balanced. So we must learn to understand our own characters and be confident enough to believe in our value.

Self-knowledge involves recognizing the scope in your life for change and development. Contrary to what you may feel, no one is completely trapped in the way they are now. We all have some choices about the way we look, move, speak, and conduct our daily lives and personal relationships. These can make a fundamental difference to the way we see ourselves.

The actual process of change involves considerable courage and resolve, and it does not happen instantly. Most of us can gain or regain control of our actions and become stronger individuals once we recognize that habit is mainly to blame for the way we become trapped in false roles. This means assessing both your negative and positive qualities, accepting your faults as well as your strengths, and trying to achieve a balanced integration of both.

It is important to recognize, however, that change is not always an easy process and can sometimes even be painful.

Do not set yourself up for disappointment by making impossible demands on yourself or others. Letting yourself off the hook and becoming more assertive can be difficult, but these skills will help you to develop the courage to stop striving to be what you are not, and grow more successfully into what you are.

Being Yourself

Everyone has good and bad points. Realizing that you are not perfect, that you are a normal human being, with insecurities and failings, is the first step to feeling good about yourself. If you have a healthy self-esteem and a positive self-image you should be able to weigh both your faults and your good points. If you find it difficult to assess your character in this way, enlist the help of a friend.

Ask him or her to give you an honest character assessment, warts and all. Write down your good and bad qualities and acknowledge them. Be proud of your good points — the special capabilities and characteristics that make you uniquely you. But remember that some good qualities have their drawbacks: virtues like modesty and humility can be deterrents to establishing self-esteem.

One of the best methods for helping you to think positively about yourself is meditation. Visualization techniques can help you to see yourself in the best possible light.

Calming Down

Mental calm and strength, the tranquil, quiet state that allows you to be perfectly centred, gives you more control over your thoughts and actions. When faced by a potentially stressful situation, you will be aware of all the options open to you. If you are strong and calm, you can stand back, become more objective, and rationalize your feelings.

Tranquillity may seem difficult to achieve if you are angry, frustrated or afraid. But if you look upon these emotions as a normal part of life, and know what causes them, it will be easier to overcome them. Try to express your feelings openly whenever you can. If you do not, you may suppress them or drive them inward, directing them at yourself. By expressing them, you will be able to dissipate them quickly and completely.

Once you have learned to express them, get used to "dropping" destructive thoughts and feelings consciously before they start to build up. If you do this, you will learn to intercept your conditioned responses to stress. People vary in their preferred techniques for breaking conditioned stress patterns.

Meditation or chanting rhythmically are all good methods of calming down if you can escape to the appropriate place. Lying on the floor, concentrating on the weight of your limbs and the central pull of gravity is also very calming.

But other diversion exercises, which you can do sitting down, are just as effective. Sit down calmly, put your hands firmly on a table, and say "stop" loudly.

Keep your knees uncrossed, your body relaxed, and breathe slowly and rhythmically.

Ask yourself what sort of a person you are and think about character traits like these – are you Calm, Animated, Type A, Type B, Thoughtful, Impetuous, Intellectual, Practical, Leader, Follower, Conventional, Unconventional, Realistic, Idealistic, Solitary, Gregarious, Quiet, Talkative, City, Country, Religious, Agnostic? You are unlikely to be wholly one extreme or the other – few people have characters that are made up entirely of extremes. Write down your profile and you will be able to see very easily your characteristics and abilities.

Focus your gaze on any object in your environment. It can be anything: your left thumb, a pencil, or a bowl of sugar. Observe all its aspects in minute detail. Become aware of its smell and texture. Lose yourself completely in it. Silently describe it and your relationship to it, over and over to yourself until you are lost in a fantasy. After five minutes you should feel calm and balanced.

Assuming Control

Even if you do not have much control over events that take place around you at work, at home, and in your relationships, you do have a choice as to how you react to them. Look for the positive aspects of any event or situation, no matter how stressful or unpleasant. Try to learn or gain something from the situation. You may feel trapped because you have not examined the choices you have of responding differently.

Simply refusing to lose your temper, or to get tearful or worried can help you gain control. You should also examine your past patterns of reaction. Many of these may have become totally automatic and irrational. Anxiety, for example, is a rehearsal of a situation that will probably never happen. Our attitude to stress, not stress itself, can cause us to feel victimized.

Each time a stressful event occurs and you start getting anxious or losing your temper, give yourself a control test. Sit down on your own for a few minutes and make yourself aware of your pulse, breathing and muscle tension. Then hold your breath for ten seconds, and exhale loudly and explosively. Do this a few times, then breathe normally and smile. As you gain control over your innermost responses you will be able to act more positively and you will find it easier to feel good about yourself.

If you find it hard to think positively about your character, list everything you can do—from the simplest thing to the most complicated. Cook, maintain accounts, drive, garden, put up shelves, type, paint and draw, play a musical instrument or play a sport? You may be surprised at the range of your abilities.

The Art of Relating

A close and loving relationship is the most fundamental of all human needs.

Our capacity for self-expression, and our happiness and emotional security depend closely on the way we relate to others. Few of us manage to live alone happily for any length of time unless we suppress many basic needs and desires.

Building long-lasting and happy relationships have become one of the major challenges of our age. The modern nuclear family, unlike the large families of the past, lacks the supportive network of sibling groups and neighbouring relatives. So it must depend far more on its own resources. Other styles of relationship, the single-parent family, and the extended family of several couples or individuals, also rely on strong internal resources for lasting success and fulfilment.

The changing social role of women has brought about profound changes in modern relationships. Women suffer stress as a result of working both in their job and at home. Working mothers suffer guilt about leaving their children to go out to work. Working not because you want to, but because you need to augment the family income also puts strains on your relationship with your partner and children. Men can fall prey to stress as a result of feeling undermined in their former role of the bread-earner.

To make our relationships work, we need to adapt to changing circumstances and to reassess the traditional guidelines and values of marriage. The expectations we have from ourselves and our partners, and of relationships in general, are now far greater than they were in the past.

Sexual satisfaction, emotional and intellectual fulfilment, and compatibility of interests, attitudes, and ambitions are what many of us search for in the ideal relationship. This motivates us to work at achieving richer, more fulfilling and equally balanced partnerships based as much on friendship and intellectual equality, as on sexual attraction and romantic love.

Yet it also makes us more critical and less tolerant when we fail to find satisfaction. Placing too many demands on our partner or having unrealistically high expectations of marriage, is a root cause of domestic strife and marital breakdown.

It is after all unrealistic to expect any one person to satisfy all of our needs and desires. Unless we can learn when and how to compromise we may place an intolerable strain on even the most loving and supportive of partners. The guilt and sense of inadequacy that stem from not being able to fulfil our partner's every want and need may in turn cause us strain and anguish.

Fortunately, we possess excellent resources for making the best of our relationships. Frankness and honesty between the sexes have never been greater than they are today. We possess more freedom and greater resources to work at our relationships, by openly expressing our needs, finding mutually acceptable areas of compromise, and achieving a fair balance of give and take. Using these resources, we should be able to get the best out of our relationships, complementing each other's strengths and accepting each other's limitations.

The Art of Working

Work dominates our lives. Most people work eight hours a day. Add to this, the time spent travelling to and from work, preparing and cleaning up, and overtime, and the total is often far greater. Work and work-related activities account for the major part of our waking hours for five or six days a week.

Our society is founded on the work ethic. This tends to make our attitude to work stoical and serious. We put in long hours, and we often silently suffer uncomfortable working conditions. We also tend to seek promotion as an emblem of success rather than a means of fulfilment, and to link our self-esteem with our earning power. Happiness still comes somewhat low on most people's lists of work priorities, but work-related stress is increasingly recognized today as a major cause of illness and mental breakdown.

Fortunately, our view of work is starting to change. Our demands and expectations are centred not only on pay and working conditions but now also on the quality of work and job satisfaction. Working also gives us a sense of belonging and purpose. In a society built on commerce and industry, the work we do, defines our role, thereby strengthening our sense of identity and conferring responsibility.

In ideal circumstances our work can broaden the scope of our lives. When satisfaction and fulfilment are high, when we enjoy the job we do and do it well, the challenges and opportunities afforded by giving of our best can encourage us to grow and develop as human beings. Recognition of our talents is therefore central to job satisfaction. The other ingredients of job satisfaction depend on the individual. For some people, security is the most important element, for others, it is the freedom to set their own targets.

Faced with increased work stress (and the phenomenon of *burnout* at all levels of the workforce), more and more employers are beginning to restructure their working methods, rethink their company policy and improve the communications and relations between management and workers. One solution is to give employees more control, which helps to avoid feelings of frustration.

Too little work, and the boredom and frustration resulting from unemployment, also cause stress. The best solution here is to learn self-discipline to prevent the drift into purposelessness.

But the structure of employment and the way we work is beginning to change. Redundancy, unemployment, and shorter working days are increasingly common, and have their benefits as well as their drawbacks.

More emphasis on leisure time and improved quality of life is causing us to revalue both our job expectations and our style of working. A shorter working day, automation, flexitime, job sharing and the use of computer links offer a range of new working styles. They also indicate a new and welcome humanization of the overall concept of work.

A freer, more open system of communication and improved working relations lead us inevitably towards greater say and control over how our working lives are run. These are essential changes to strive for, if we are to experience less stress and enjoy happier, more harmonious working lives.

Planning Your Time

Punctuated by sunrise and sunset, light and darkness, our daily or circadian cycle dominates our lives. It regulates our periods of sleep, hunger and activity, by controlling mood, mental alertness, and bodily functions. The way the body clock is set varies from person to person. This fact explains why some people operate at their best early in the day, others late at night.

Whatever we are doing, time is a precious commodity. Fitting in all your tasks, commitments, and leisure activities into your waking hours can create time shortages. The longer and more demanding your work schedule and home life is, the greater is the risk of becoming a victim of what stress researchers call *hurry sickness*.

Those most likely to suffer are highly stressed Type-A personalities, for whom the stress of time-urgency tends to be self-generated. The immediate consequences of this type of behaviour are familiar: undone jobs pile up or are completed late, deadlines loom, tempers are lost, and anxiety and panic ensue.

Work is not the only thing that suffers when this happens. Relationships and home life become subject to the same panic pressures and time shortages. Resentment at too much time spent working, too little relaxing and enjoying the company of family and friends, is bound to limit the amount of satisfaction you derive from life in general. But if you have too much time to spare, as a result of unemployment or underwork, you are also likely to have problems. The lack of mental and physical stimulus can lead to feelings of depression and isolation.

To avoid these traps you must be able to control your relationships to time. The most effective way of doing this involves very careful planning: assessing your capabilities and working out schedules incorporating leisure activities also. The result should be that you will be able to get more done in the hours available to you, with a better balance of work, home, and leisure activities.

Nutrition and Exercise

Food is the fuel that we take into our bodies and exercise creates the energy that uses up this fuel. They create a delicate balance. If you exercise too little and eat too much, you risk becoming overweight, while eating too little and exercising too much also cause health problems. Until quite recently, our life-style allowed our energy input and output to be balanced automatically. We burnt up our calories to fuel body warmth and physical work.

In today's consumer society most of us enjoy ample food, warmth and comfort with minimum physical effort. Sedentary jobs, labour-saving devices in the home, automation in industry and motorized transport have led many of us to become less physically active, while relative affluence encourages us to follow a diet dominated by rich and fattening foods. The balance of energy supply and demand has been badly upset.

Overweight can lead to health hazards when linked with a highly stressed, Type A personality profile, having disorders such as high blood pressure and high blood cholesterol, or habits such as smoking or drinking. It puts an added strain on the heart, lungs and other internal organs, with the effect of sapping energy, and lowering stamina.

Regular exercise and a well-balanced and nutritious diet can control your weight. Exercise is also an ideal outlet for accumulated tension, aggression and frustration, and neutralizes mental as well as muscular stress. People who exercise regularly claim some of the following benefits: improved sleep, fewer headaches, fewer stress-related aches and pains, a greater sense of inner calm, improved mental clarity and concentration and greater physical stamina.

Recent research shows that powerful brain chemicals are released during vigorous exercise. These are called endorphins – morphine-like substances associated with happiness and well-being. This is why exercise can often dispel negative mental states such as depression or anxiety.

Assessing your diet

A varied, well-balanced diet is a basic cornerstone of healthy living. There is considerable controversy over exactly what makes up a well-balanced diet. But the potential hazards of eating very large quantities of refined and processed food, animal fats, dairy produce, and sugar are well documented, as are the health-giving properties of fresh fruits, vegetables, salads, grains and wholefoods.

There are also certain foods that affect your mood. Eaten in excess these can influence your stress level. So look at your diet and see if there are any deficiencies and avoid junk foods and high-calorie snacks that give an instant energy high and damage general health.

Dietary Deficiencies

Losing out on essential nutrients can be due to several reasons. Make sure your food is fresh. Once it gets to the shops, fresh food has an extremely short shelf-life – nutrients such as vitamin C and the vitamin B group are rapidly destroyed or depleted through processing, storage, heat and light. Overcooking also destroys nutrients. Eat as many raw vegetables as you can, and if you do cook them, do so minimally. Buy organically grown vegetables. If you think your diet is deficient, look at the chart to see which elements might be missing.

Symptoms of Deficiency	
Symptom	**Deficiency**
Tiredness, anaemia	Lack of iron, vitamin B12
Colds, flu, infection	Lack of vitamin C
Cramps, irritability, PMT	Lack of B complex vitamins, calcium, magnesium
Dry skin, eczema, skin sores, bleeding gums	Lack of vitamin A, vitamin C, linoleic acid, polyunsaturated fat, zinc
Brittle, weak bones, aches in joints	Lack of vitamin D, calcium
Fatigue, weight gain	Lack of iodine (i.e. Thyroid imbalance)
Fluid retention (oedema)	Lack of potassium; excess salt
Migraine, dizziness, irritability, depression	Low blood sugar, insufficient protein and complex carbohydrates; excess sugar and sweet foods.
Constipation, liverishness, irritable bowel syndrome	Lack of fibre; excess of refined, processed foods

Food and Mood

Some foods influence emotions and behaviour patterns. The immediate effect of some is pleasant: alcohol, for example, makes most people feel relaxed quickly. But if you consume too much alcohol, like the other substances in the chart given, you can reduce your body's ability to withstand stress.

Food Supplements

Tailor your diet to your life-style. If you are under a great deal of stress or emotional trauma, you are likely to need more of the B-complex vitamins, vitamin C, and minerals such as zinc, which the body uses up more quickly under stress. This also applies to people who smoke, drink a lot of alcohol, take antibiotics or are on the contraceptive pill.

MOOD FOODS

Food	Physical Effects	Adverse Reactions
Caffeine (in coffee, tea, aspirin, cola drinks)	Mimics stress arousal: directs stimulus of nervous system; increased alertness; stimulates heart, kidneys, adrenal glands; dilates blood vessels	Irritates kidneys; headaches, lethargy, irritability, muscular fatigue, nervousness, palpitations; these effects are especially bad when excessive intake is followed by withdrawal of tea or coffee
Sugar,	Floods bloodstream giving instant energy high for short time and temporarily relieving physical tiredness.	Adrenal glands overworked, making them less effective at regulating blood sugar levels; indorsed tiredness, depression, irritability.

Cont...

Salt	Works with potassium to regulate the body's fluid balance.	High blood pressure, nervousness, irritability when taken in excess; stimulates adrenal glands, stimulating stress arousal
Tryptophan (amino acid present in chicken, fish, milk, bananas, pasta, rice)	Increases manufacture of the brain chemical serotonin, encouraging relaxation and sleepiness.	Drowsiness, if too many foods rich in tryptophan are eaten during the day.
Alcohol	Dilates blood vessels, raises blood sugar levels, relaxes body and mind, stimulates appetite and digestion.	When taken in excess: liver damage, blood sugar problems, impaired judgement and brain function, poor co-ordination, depression, dependence on alcohol.

Food Supplements	
Supplement	**Condition**
Vitamin C	Colds; after excessive intake of alcohol; when smoking cigarettes.
Vitamin B6	PMT; taking the contraceptive pill, antibiotics; times of tension and prolonged stress.
Oil of evening primrose	PMT; during excessive intake of alcohol; cigarette smoking; eczema.
Lysine	Cold sores, eczema, psoriasis.
Iron plus vitamin B12	Tiredness; iron-deficiency anaemia; heavy periods.
Dolomite, calcium, magnesium, vitamin B6	Insomnia, irritability, muscular cramp.
Brewer's yeast (rich in B complex vitamins)	Stress, excess alcohol intake, smoking cigarettes, contraceptive pills, antibiotics.
Feverfew	Migraine
Zinc plus vitamin E	Burns, wounds.

The Stress-free Diet

The idea of changing your diet to strengthen your body's defences against stress is not a new one. Fasting, purification régimes, and the dietary principles of yoga all aim to cleanse the body, eliminate harmful toxins, and allow the internal organs to rest and recuperate. The result should be a stronger body and increased energy – both mental and physical.

A healthy diet should consist of several elements. Among the most important are fresh fruits, vegetables, and fibre. If you eat meat, make sure it is lean, or remove the fat before cooking. Many of the foods we rely on at times of stress and tiredness are themselves stress-inducing. But there are healthy alternatives to most of them, many of which are more palatable than their stress-inducing counterparts.

Your attitude is as important for your health as what you actually eat. Always put time aside to enjoy your food and eat slowly, savouring each mouthful. Do not eat while reading, cooking, talking on the telephone, or working. If you tend to eat more when you are depressed, watch out for the signs and try doing something completely different—do some exercise, relax with a book, or visit a friend. And, above all, whenever you eat—enjoy your food.

Healthy Alternatives

Food Group	Foods	Alternatives
Sweet foods	Biscuits, jams, cakes, chocolates, sweets, sugared cereals, cocoa, sweet drinks, honey, relishes, puddings, pies, processed foods containing hidden sugar.	Sugar-free jam, apple butter, apple and pear spread, blackstrap molasses, muesli, aspartamine sugar substitute, carob chocolate substitute, raisins, dates, figs, dried fruit, fresh fruit juices.
Saturated/ animal fats	Fatty red meat, pork, bacon, sausages, hamburgers, lard, suet dripping, hard margarine, full-fat milk,	Lean chicken, fish, game, polyunsaturated vegetable oils and margarines, skimmed milk, low-fat yoghurt, cottage cheese, goat's milk cheese.

Contd...

	cream, full-fat yoghurt, fried food, butter, full-fat cheese, hidden fats in sauces, dressings, soups.	
Processed/ refined foods	White flour, white rice, white bread, pre-packed foods, all foods in the "sweet" category.	Brown rice, wholewheat flour, rye, barley, corn, oats, buckwheat; wholemeal bread, pasta, and rice; pulses, beans, wholegrain cereals.
Salt	Chips, crisps, salted nuts, processed foods that use salt as a preservative.	Raw unsalted nuts, pumpkin seeds, sunflower seeds, raw vegetables, seaweed.
Caffeine	Coffee, tea, cola drinks, some painkillers.	Herbal teas, decaffeinated coffee, dandelion coffee, fresh vegetables and fruit juices, spring water.

Avoiding Unhealthy Foods

The modern diet contains several groups of foods which, though unhealthy, many of us feel we cannot do without. There are healthy alternatives to most of these. Many taste similar to the foods they replace; most are actually more appetizing – try the healthy alternatives and you will probably end up preferring them on grounds of taste alone. Beware of unhealthy foods when you are eating out and the choice is limited. At parties, steer clear of nuts, cheese, biscuits, and canapés. Instead, fill up with vegetables, such as celery, radishes and carrot sticks.

Relaxation Techniques

Relaxation is the most natural activity in the world. Animals retain an in-built capacity for alternating periods of physical tension with regular states of relaxation in a way that we humans have long forgotten. Look at the way a cat stretches its limbs, or sensuously arches its back, how a dog yawns and flops on its back, its paws hanging loose.

For relaxation to be effective, we need to banish tension from both mind and body. Ideally speaking a good night's sleep should perform this function. But there is no guarantee that it will, and although we do spend a lot of our sleeping time – though by no means all of it – in a relaxed state, sleep alone is not enough. Today, when we are continuously bombarded by stress-inducing stimuli, we need to develop our skills in conscious relaxation as much as possible.

Many people do not realise how unrelaxed they really are. If you have started to ignore the build-up of strain and tension in your limbs, joints, and muscles, and fail to defuse these physical stresses when they begin to affect your mind and body, you will gradually begin to store that tension in various parts of your body.

Allowing hidden tension to increase and take hold of your body will inevitably affect the way that you feel and how you function, since a tense body is less efficient and co-ordinated than a relaxed one. You will also start to feel the physical effects of stress—a broad gamut of aches and pains from migraine headaches to back pain.

There are two immediate advantages of learning to relax. Firstly, as you begin to practise relaxation techniques you will become aware at once of the areas of your body that are most prone to stiffness and pain. This can help to keep you on your guard against factors that may exacerbate the strain—your posture, your furniture, the shoes and clothes you wear, and the way you use your body in general.

Secondly, you will simply feel much better—almost immediately. Five minutes spent loosening your face, neck and shoulder muscles may banish a headache and leave you feeling calm and refreshed, while twenty minutes' deeper relaxation can rest and revive both mind and body as much as two hours' sleep.

Conscious relaxation consists of learning systematically to empty the mind and muscles of stress and external stimuli through a series of deliberately disciplined, progressive exercises.

Relaxation and the Body

When we are truly relaxed, very definite and measurable changes take place in the body. These changes distinguish relaxation from the opposite states of tension or arousal.

Some of the most significant changes are triggered by the two branches of the autonomic nervous system. The sympathetic branch of the nervous system slows down. This branch controls body temperature, digestion, heart rate, respiratory rate, blood flow and pressure and muscular tension. Conversely, the opposite, parasympathetic, branch of the nervous system comes increasingly into play. This lowers oxygen consumption and reduces the following bodily functions: carbon dioxide elimination, heart and respiratory rates, blood pressure, blood lactate and blood cortisol levels. It also reduces muscle tone, and activates the internal organs to work more efficiently. These bodily changes are collectively referred to by doctors as the "relaxation response". This is the reverse of the aroused "fight or flight" response with which we react to stress.

Relaxation and the Brain

The activity of the brain can provide vital information about how relaxed you are. The brain emits four different types of waves, each with its own characteristic rhythm. These are beta, the ordinary conscious day-to-day rhythms; delta, present when we sleep and dream; theta, which reflect a withdrawn, dream-like state; and alpha, which are associated with deep physical relaxation and emotional tranquillity, when the mind is calm yet still awake and alert.

Very deep relaxation and meditation induce a predominance of alpha and theta rhythms, indicating a state of harmony. It is possible to measure these waves by using biofeedback equipment, and many doctors and therapists use this technique as a way of monitoring how relaxed we are.

Recent research also suggests that among the biochemical changes triggered by relaxation, there is an increase in the body's manufacture of certain mood-altering chemicals (known as neurotransmitters). In particular, the body's production of serotonin, which is associated principally with feelings of calmness and happiness, is increased.

Choosing Relaxation Exercises

The exercises illustrated in this chapter are simple to learn and to carry out. They are designed to be done either as a complete top-to-toe series, or singly, depending on how much time you have and what your individual requirements are. Some will help you get rid of tension in specific parts of your body. Others will give a more general relaxation, producing a calming effect like that of meditation.

Relaxation exercises are an ideal way of waking up and flexing the muscles after sleep, to ease away early-morning stiffness. You can also use these exercises as a mid-morning or afternoon break to relieve tension at work, while in the evening they can help dispel fatigue. Another way to use these exercises, especially the more strenuous ones like those for the neck, back and shoulders, is to do them at night to help you to go to sleep. If you do them regularly, they will eventually become second nature and essential to your mental and physical well-being.

If you are too busy to do the whole series, or if you feel that you need to relax one particular part of your body, then you will still find that doing one or two exercises will help you relax. For example, if tension

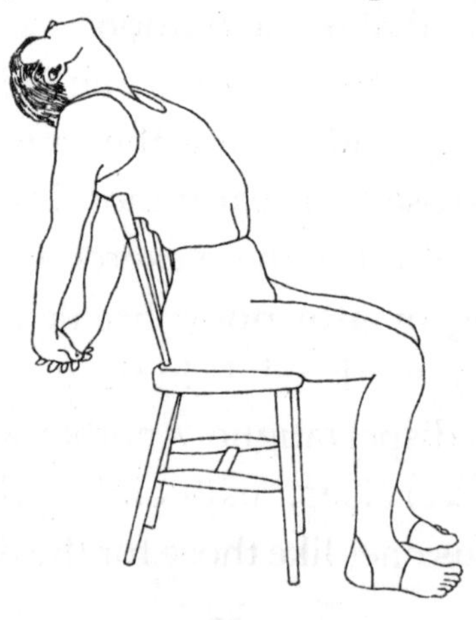

is building up in your head and neck, you may choose to do only the exercises that cover this area. If you feel generally tense, but do not have time to do all the exercises, try one or more of the general exercises.

One of the most effective exercises is to lie on the floor or sit on a chair and progressively tense and let go, stretch and release each and every part of the body. This exercise is deeply relaxing and helps you to recognise and distinguish between the different sensations of tension and relaxation. Allow plenty of time for this exercise and concentrate your mind on feelings of heaviness and warmth in your limbs, while keeping your breathing smooth. Whether you do one exercise or a whole series, remember that you will obtain the most lasting benefit if you exercise regularly, at the same time every day.

Head and Neck Exercises

Tension can lodge in the back of the neck and this in turn causes constriction of the small muscles and blood vessels of the scalp, temples and hairline if you have to work at a desk for long periods, or if you spend a lot of time standing and talking. Headaches and migraine are obvious warnings. Tightness of the throat, eye strain, numbness, and cricks in the neck are also symptoms of this type of tension.

Head Rolls

Roll your head slowly clockwise and then counter-clockwise, three times each way, allowing it to drop heavily.

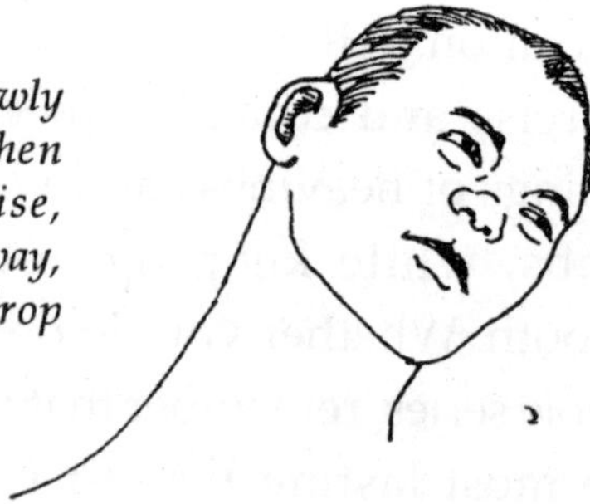

Head and Neck

Head rolls and neck stretches ease away deep-rooted tension. To make them more effective, practise them as slowly as possible to maximize the stretch. Moving the head too rapidly when you are tense, can increase stiffness and cause twinges and cricks. Each time you drop the head, feel its complete weight and allow your jaw to open and your eyes to close so that the relaxing effects are increased.

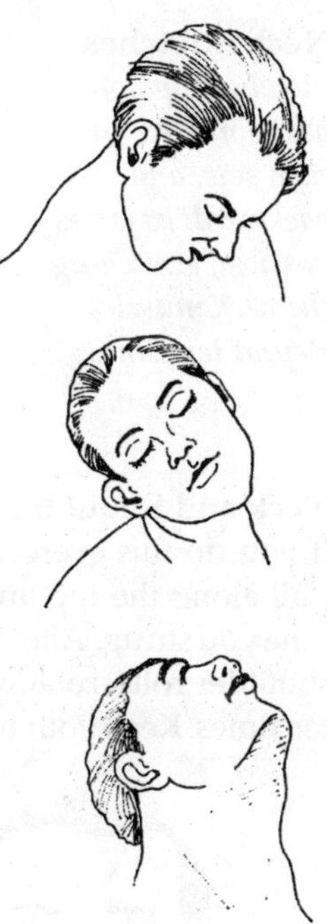

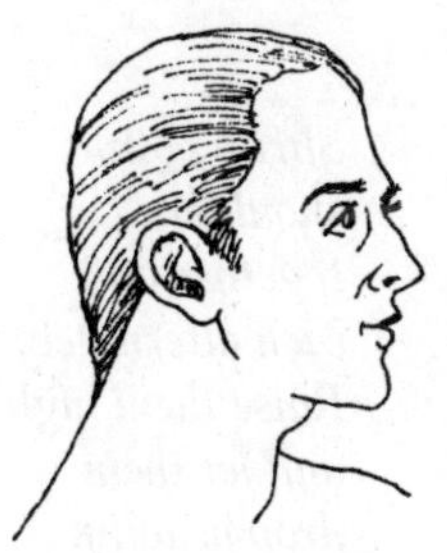

Turning the Head

Keeping your head level, turn it side to side ten times slowly, then ten times more quickly.

Neck Stretches
Slowly drop your head forward, to each side, and backward, as far as possible, stretching the neck muscles. Repeat ten times.

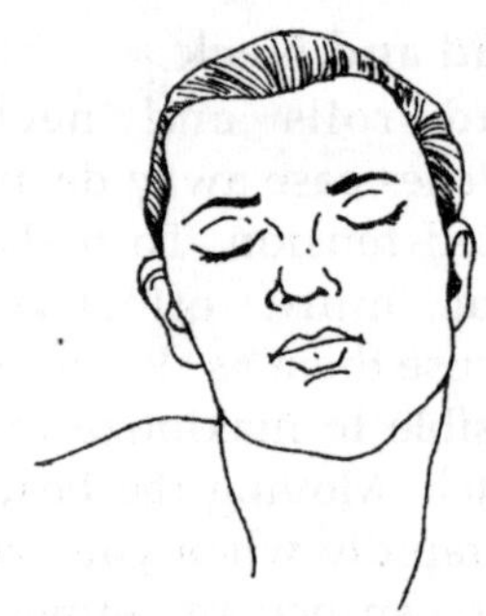

Neck and Shoulders
If you do this exercise correctly you should feel the pull along the top and back of your shoulders each time you shrug. Alternate shrugging movements with shoulder rolls, rotating shoulders back then forward ten times. Keep your hands and arms completely limp.

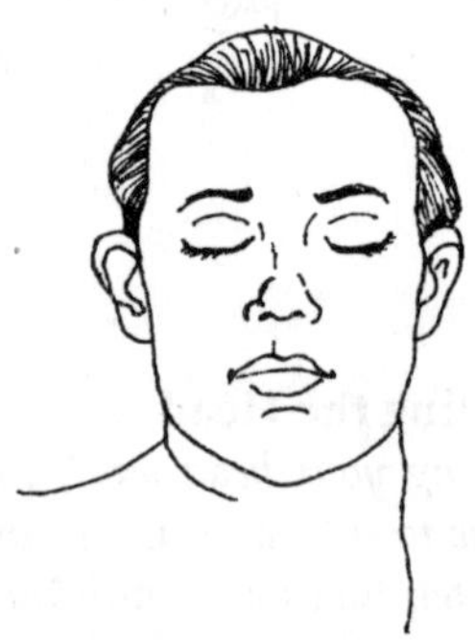

Shrug both shoulders together and each alternately. Raise them high and let them drop heavily.

Neck, Back and Shoulder Exercises

Shoulder tension and backache are very common and have many causes. Deskbound jobs and poor posture are two of the main factors. Heavy lifting can also result in back strain, especially if you bend forward with straight legs to pick up heavy objects off the floor.

Women who wear very high heels most of the day, or regularly carry heavy shopping bags with one arm, risk distorting the alignment of back and shoulders. Swap bags from side to side and wear the strap of your shoulder bag diagonally across your upper body. Release tension from shoulders, neck and back as soon as you feel it.

Neck and Shoulders

There is no set time or rhythm for these upper body exercises. Do them as slowly as you wish, and stay bent over as long as you feel you need to relax. Try to feel the contrast between the upward stretch and the heaviness of a completely relaxed upper body as you drop forward from the hips.

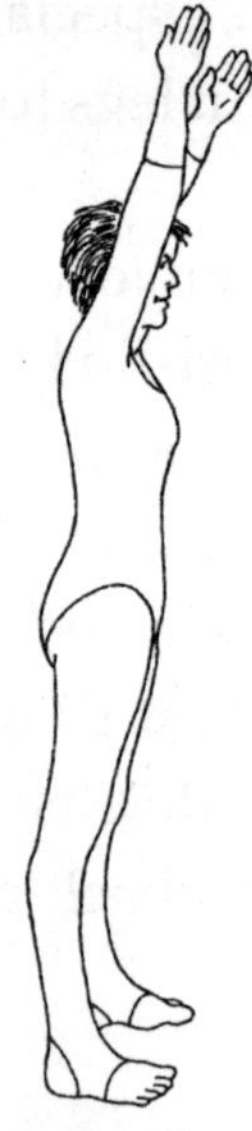

1. *Stand upright, your feet about twelve inches apart and parallel, your arms stretched above your head.*

2. *Allow your upper body to drop forward from the hips, keeping the knees relaxed or slightly bent. Let the arms, head, and shoulders hang relaxed for up to forty seconds.*

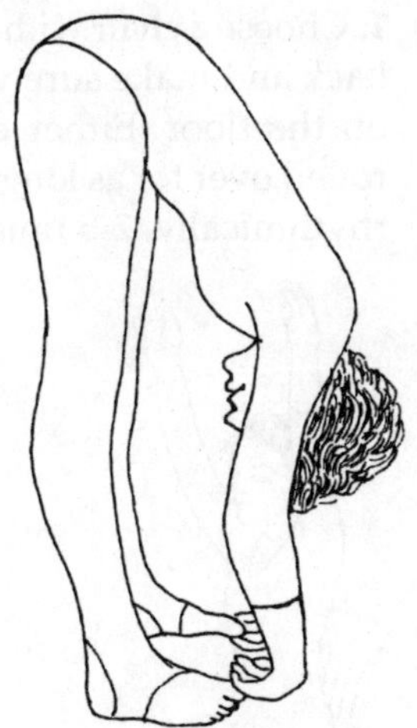

3. *Shake out the arms and shoulders, nod and shake the head, then slowly raise the body. Repeat a few times.*

1. Choose a chair with a firm seat and a hard, upright back and make sure you can place your feet firmly on the floor. Either do the exercise once, staying rolled over for as long as you can, or practise it more rhythmically, 2-5 times.

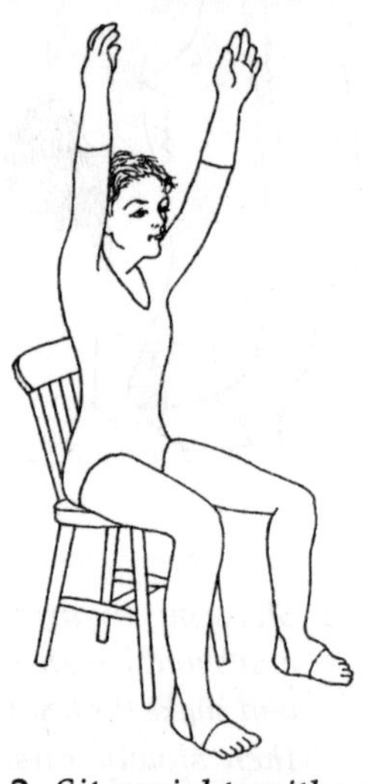

2. *Sit upright, with your lower back supported by the chair, and stretch your arms and trunk upward. Keep your feet parallel about 20 ins (50 cm) apart.*

3. *Drop your body forward, trying to keep your buttocks firmly on the seat. Let your head and arms hang heavily.*

Backstretch

For this exercise you need a chair with a firm, upright back that comes up to shoulder-blade level. Do not worry if at first you cannot stretch back very far. As tension and tightness in the shoulders and upper arms eases, you will be able to stretch further and gain more pliability. Do the movements slowly but with no set rhythm.

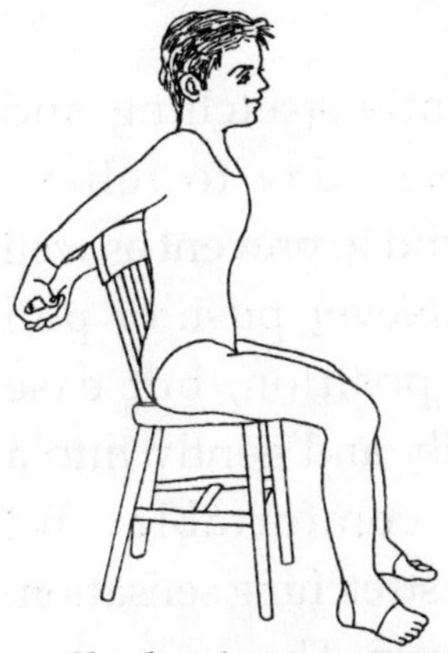

1. *Slowly raise your arms behind the back of the chair clasping the hands firmly. Squeeze your shoulder blades together.*

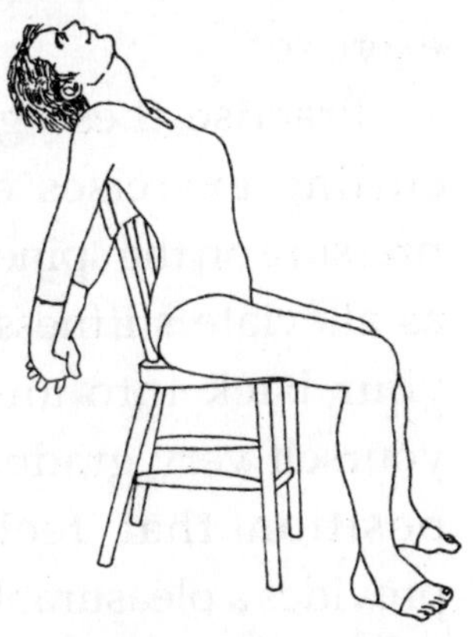

2. *Gradually lean backward, arching your upper back over the chair. Try to keep your arms at the same angle to your back.*

Spine and Lower Back Exercises

Lower backache is by far the most common back problem. It can be due to incorrect posture, badly designed furniture, beds that are too hard or too soft, pregnancy, menstruation, weight gain, and lack of exercise.

Practise these gentle stretching and curling exercises every day to relieve pressure on the spine and to prevent as well as alleviate stiffness. Never push or pull your back into any position, but ease yourself very gradually and gently into a position that feels comfortable and provides a pleasurable stretching sensation. Stop if you feel any strain. These exercises also provide a good warm up and cool down before and after a more hectic exercise session.

Foetal roll

Most of us naturally adopt the foetal, curled-up posture if we have a tense or aching back. But pulling the knees upto the chest gives a fuller stretch and relieves tension faster. Do this exercise either on the floor or in bed before going to sleep. You can also do it on waking up if your back gets stiff at this time.

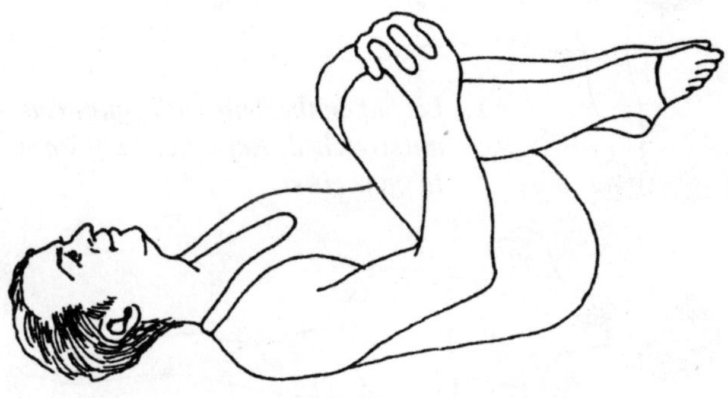

Lie on the floor and draw your knees up towards your chest. Hold them in position with your hands and rest in this pose for as long as you feel comfortable.

Backstretch

Gaining sufficient flexibility to do this exercise takes time and perseverance until the muscles become used to being stretched. Concentrate all the time on relaxing your hips, inner thighs, and upper back muscles.

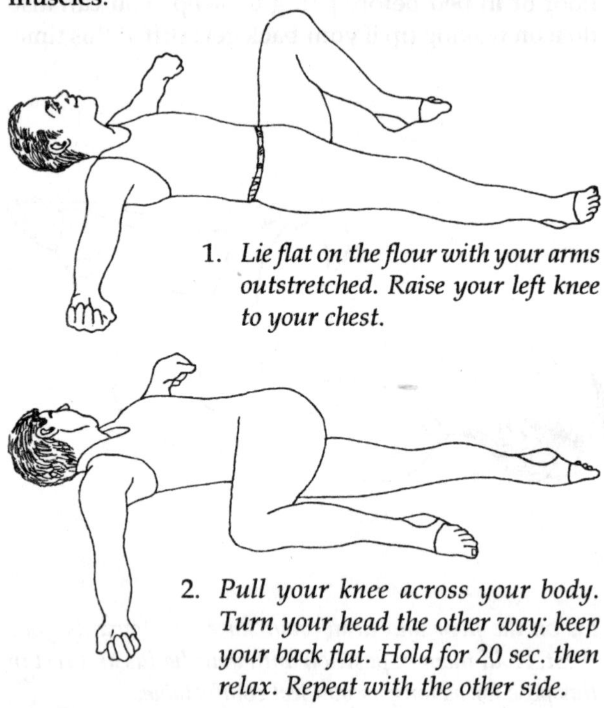

1. *Lie flat on the flour with your arms outstretched. Raise your left knee to your chest.*

2. *Pull your knee across your body. Turn your head the other way; keep your back flat. Hold for 20 sec. then relax. Repeat with the other side.*

Warm-up

This simple technique eases tension in the lower and middle back by gently stretching the spine. It also increases the flexibility of the hip joints as well as encourages the stretch of the groin muscles. Tightness of the hips and groin automatically creates tension in the lower back and vice-versa. Do this exercise in your own time and do not rush the forward stretch. Grasp the ankles and pull yourself over very slowly and gently without straining the muscles.

1. *Sit upright, hands clasping your ankles and your knees bent.*

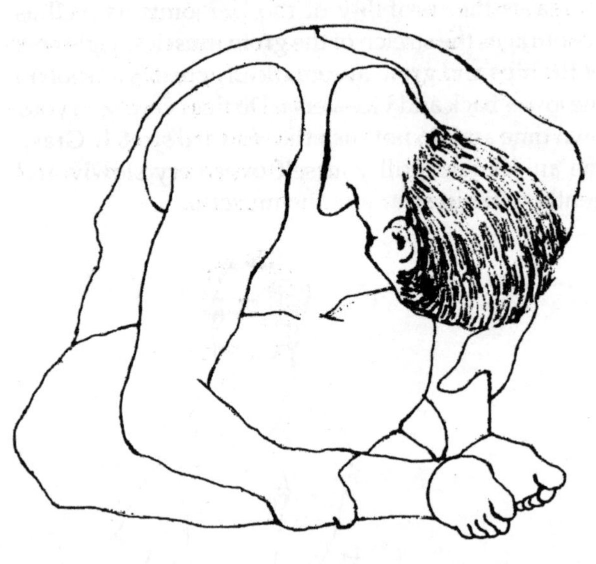

2. *Slowly bend forward. Try to place your head on your feet. Hold, then sit up. Repeat five times.*

Facing Mecca

Think of a cat when you practise this yoga-type backstretch, which is designed to relieve tension along the entire length of the spine. Your head should remain relaxed while your arms feel as if you are reaching forward as far as you can. Do not allow your bottom and lower spine to rise up and concentrate on pressing your back into the floor.

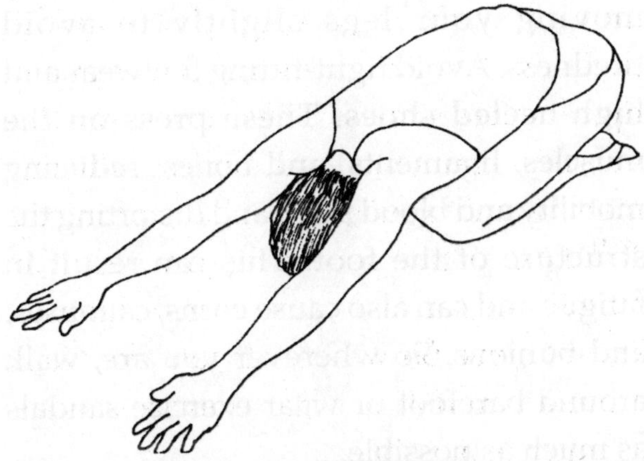

Kneel with your body upright and your arms resting at your sides. Lower your buttocks onto your heels, then pull your body forward as shown above. Rest in this pose as long as you wish.

Leg and Foot Exercises

Healthy feet, leg muscles, and knee joints are essential for balance, mobility and good posture. Unless you walk a lot or exercise regularly these can all stiffen up and lose their strength and tone.

When sitting for long periods keep moving your legs slightly to avoid tiredness. Avoid tight-fitting footwear and high-heeled shoes. These press on the muscles, ligaments, and bones, reducing mobility and blood flow, and distorting the structure of the foot. This can result in fatigue and can also cause corns, callouses, and bunions. So wherever you are, walk around barefoot or wear exercise sandals as much as possible.

Relaxing the feet

Through restrictive footwear, we tend to lose contact with the true feel of the ground. The foot muscles get cramped, leading to distortion, stiffness and aches, which affects our balance and movement. Through foot and leg exercises without shoes and socks, savour the contact of bare flesh on carpet or wood and concentrate on keeping the toes as far apart as possible. Wiggle them around and separate them into a fan shape from time to time to increase mobility and relieve stiffness. Do this exercise slowly and rhythmically to exercise your legs and feet.

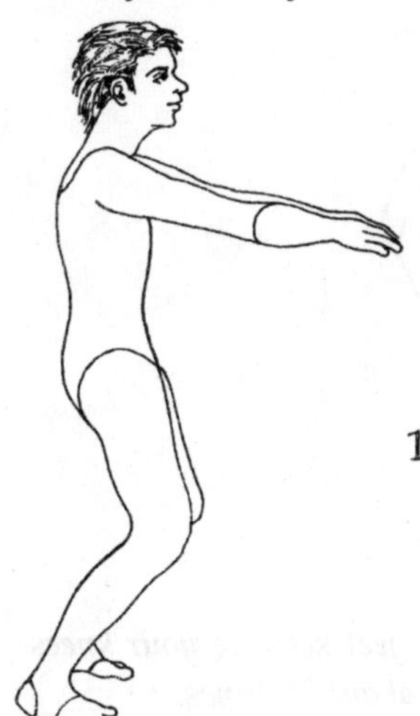

1. *Stand with your knees slightly bent and your feet about twelve inches apart and parallel. Keep your arms outstretched.*

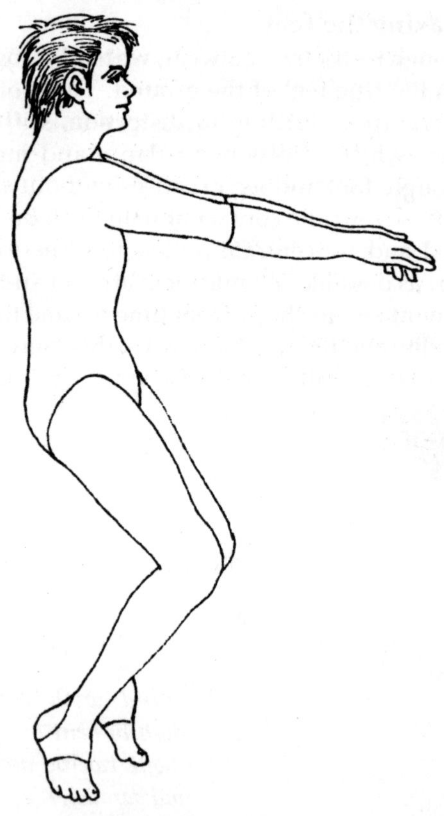

2. *Roll up onto the balls of the feet keeping your knees bent, then roll back. Do this about 20 times.*

Ankle rolls

Tension accumulates in the ankle joints, the front of the calves, and the foot muscles. This happens especially if you do not exercise regularly, spend a lot of time sitting or standing, or wear restricting shoes. Fluid retention, especially in women, can aggravate stiffness and discomfort in the feet. It can be caused by long-distance air travel, a faulty diet, and poor circulation. Take off your shoes and wiggle your toes then roll your ankles whenever and wherever you can.

1. *Lift your leg high in front of you, keeping your knee straight. Flex your foot, then rotate it eight times clockwise and eight times counter-clockwise*

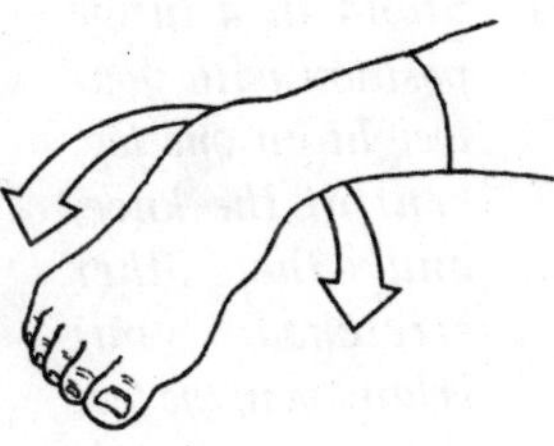

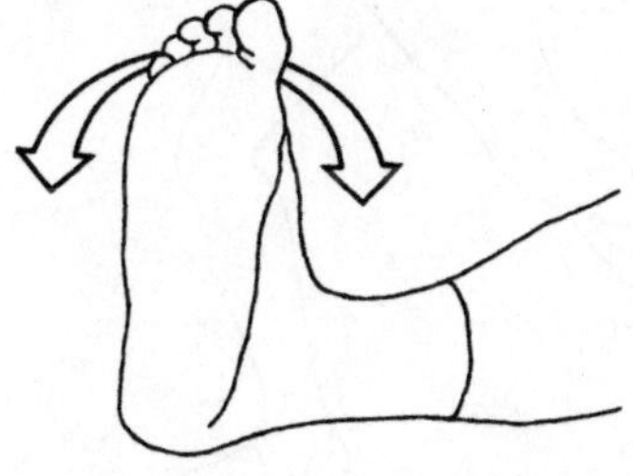

2. *Do the same rotations with your foot pointed.*

Relaxing the knees

Long periods of inactivity, tiredness, even anger and irritability, cause tension to lodge in the muscles and ligaments surrounding the knee. Leg kicks will help relax the knees. Do them barefoot or wearing gym-shoes—this will allow you to shake off the accumulated tension. Don't try to kick too high, and let the leg relax immediately after the kick.

1. *Stand in a lunge position with your weight on one leg, bent at the knee, and the other stretched out behind you, the foot flat on the ground.*

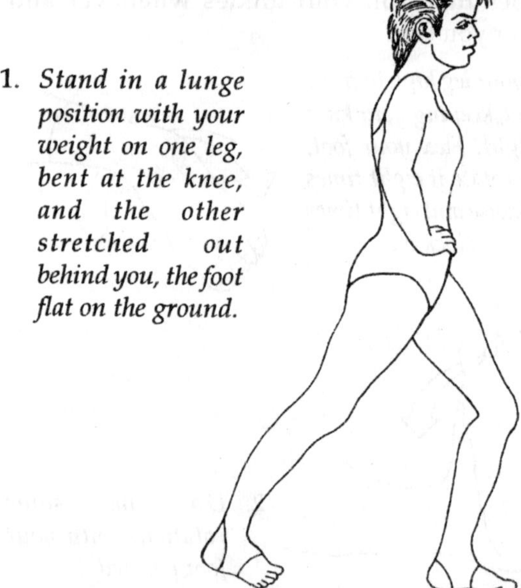

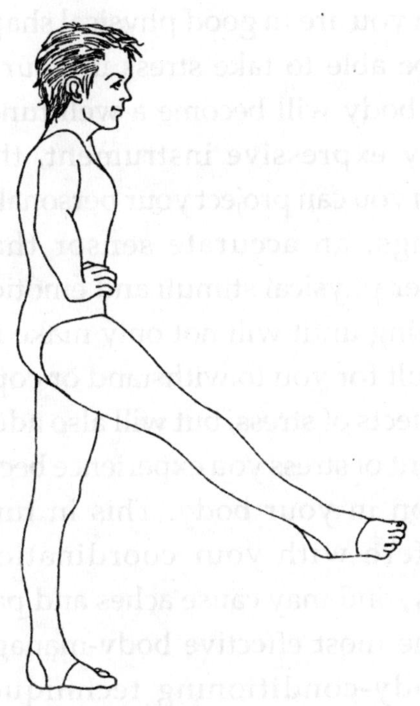

2. *Kick the extended leg forward, keeping your foot relaxed, flicking from the knee. Repeat ten times with each leg.*

Body Management

When you are in good physical shape, you will be able to take stress in your stride. Your body will become a well-tuned and highly expressive instrument, through which you can project your personality and feelings, an accurate sensor that will register physical stimuli and emotions.

Being unfit will not only make it more difficult for you to withstand or cope with the effects of stress, but will also add to the amount of stress you experience because of tension in your body. This in turn will interfere with your coordination and agility, and may cause aches and pains.

The most effective body-management or body-conditioning techniques can unburden the human body of years of accumulated stresses and strains reflected by faulty posture and lack of physical awareness. But they have other benefits. They can remove the straitjacketing effects of past illnesses, emotional shocks, or traumas, and help you identify unresolved negative emotions such as anger or depression which are often locked into certain parts of the body, distorting and limiting its freedom of movement.

These techniques also help to improve your posture. This is something to which most people are largely oblivious. But bad posture is guaranteed to load the body with extra tension and stress. It is revealed by shallow or erratic breathing, clumsy gestures, stilted body rhythms, and even strained facial expressions. Yet hunched shoulders, a stooped tensed back, a rigid neck and head, and a slumped abdominal area, can creep upon us unawares and become second nature.

Eventually these will lead to physical weakness and strain, and increase the risk of injury especially to the back. In fact, the back is the first part of you that suffers if you develop faulty posture.

Playing sports or exercising does not necessarily guarantee a well coordinated, relaxed body. Vigorous exercise can often work-in posture defects and accentuate isolated problems and pains.

To establish if yours is a truly well-integrated body, ask yourself whether it has these five key characteristics: strength, suppleness, agility, coordination and balance. These qualities can be cultivated by practising one of the bodywork systems or body therapies such as Medau, Feldenkrais, Pilates, T'ai chi, or Mensendieck. These systems will realign, strengthen and stretch the body within the limits of its own individual capability.

You cannot completely isolate and work on one part of the body without affecting others. Posture is a chain of cause and effect, complete with weak links and stresses. So be conscious of the entire body when exercising any part of it: all the limbs and organs are linked and interdependent, so strain and misplacement in one area of the body will inevitably be reflected in another.

Back Muscles

These exercises are designed to stretch the back muscles and those along the sides of the body. Do them very slowly and rhythmically to obtain a maximum stretch, creating a sensation of lengthening your upper body from the hip joints, buttocks, and upper thighs, all the way along your body to the arm sockets.

Backarch

Whenever practising back exercises that involve lying stretched out on the floor, concentrate on extending the spine and limbs to their fullest in order to counteract the shortening of the back muscles and prevent strain. You should also avoid hunching the shoulders, neck strain, and shortening of the neck muscles.

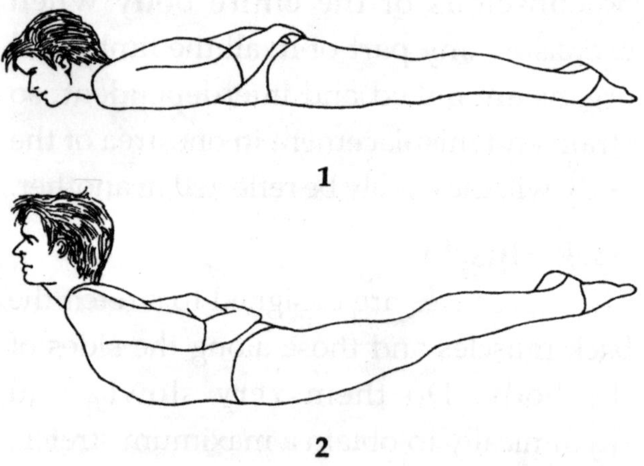

1. *Lie on your tummy as above*
2. *Clench your buttocks and raise your legs and trunk, pulling back your arms. Hold for five seconds then relax. Repeat five times.*

Backstretch

By extending your legs and arms simultaneously while lying on the floor on your tummy, you will be giving the back muscles, legs, hips and sides of your body a uniform stretch that helps to improve the all-over posture and strengthen the back. Keep your neck relaxed and fully extended and your head in alignment with your neck.

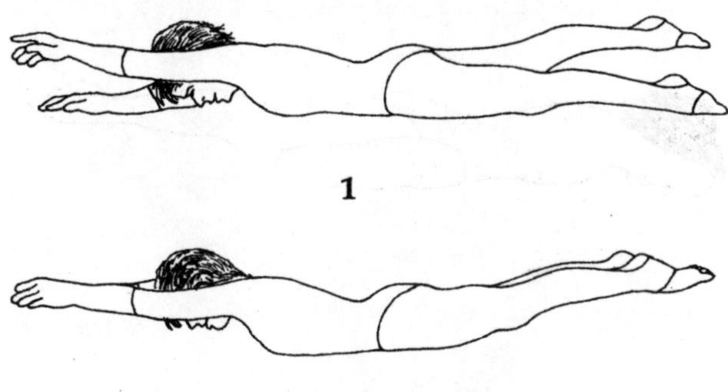

1

2

1. *Lie flat on your front and make sure your back is not arched. Raise your left arm and right leg, pulling backward and forward in opposing directions.*
2. *Repeat with the other arm and leg. Then do the exercise with both arms and legs simultaneously. Relax. Do the whole sequence five times.*

Leglift

Do not attempt this exercise if you have a lower spine injury. Using a pillow to support the hips takes the strain off the lumbar region and encourages the body to adopt the correct posture automatically. At first, do not lift the legs too high.

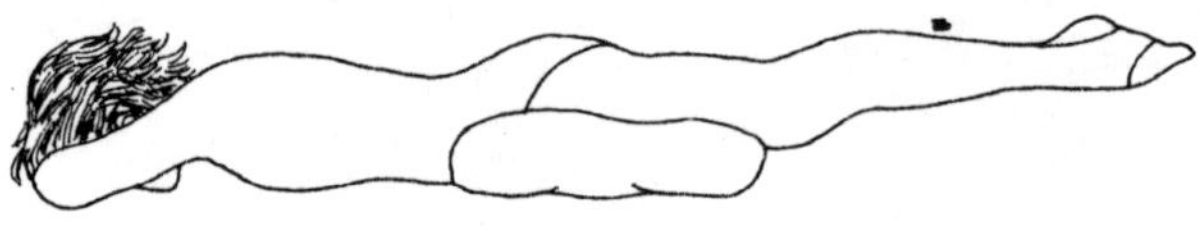

1. *Supporting your hips with a small cushion, lie down on your tummy. Rest your forehead in your clasped hands.*

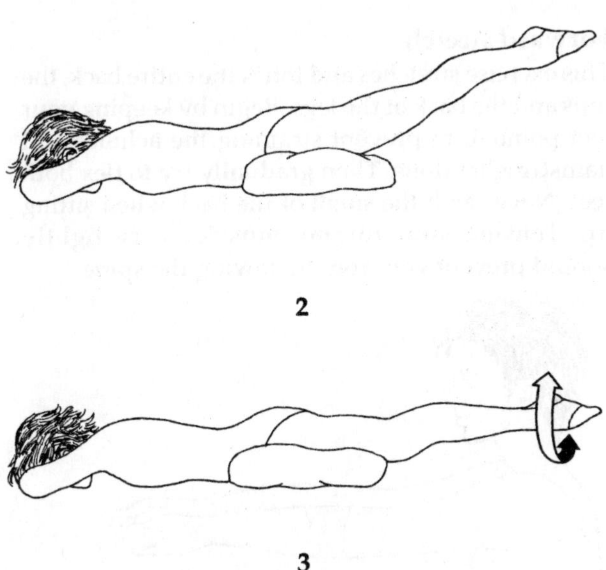

2

3

2. *Slowly lift both legs off the floor by clenching the thigh and buttock muscles.*
3. *Hold for a few seconds, then lower slowly. Repeat ten times.*

Forward stretch

This exercise stretches and tones the entire back, the hips and the back of the legs. Begin by keeping your feet pointed, to prevent straining the achilles and hamstring tendons. Then gradually try to flex both feet. Never arch the small of the back when sitting up. Tensing your tummy muscles very tightly should prevent you from hollowing the spine.

1. *Sit upright, with your legs stretched out on the floor. Hold your arms out in front.*

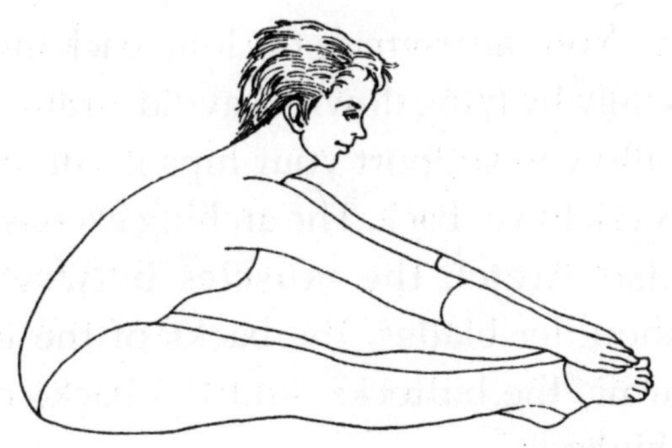

2. *With your feet pointed, slowly stretch your upper body over your legs, gripping your feet with your hands.*

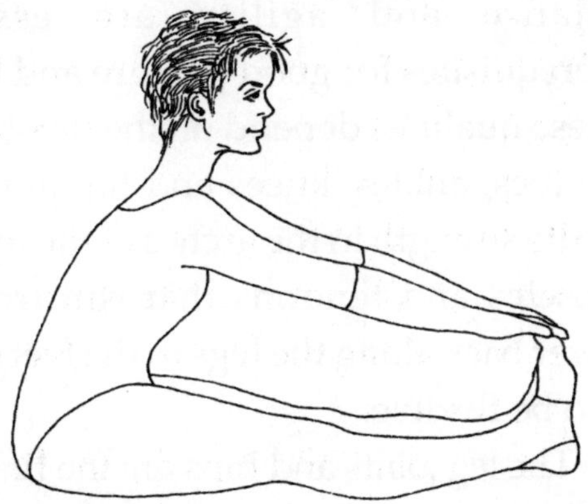

3. *Do the same with your feet flexed. Repeat each ten times.*

You can exercise the long back muscles safely by lying down to avoid strain. Use a pillow to support your hips if you have a weak lower back. The arching exercise will also stretch the muscles between the shoulder-blades, the backs of the upper arms, the buttocks, and the backs of the thighs.

Legs, Ankles and Feet

Balance and agility are essential prerequisites for good posture and fitness. These qualities depend on the flexibility of the toes, ankles, knees and hip joints and on the strength in the arches of the feet. The muscles and tendons that run from the lower back along the legs to the feet should also be flexible.

The leg joints and hips are the first areas to stiffen up through inactivity, and the weaker your leg muscles, the stiffer your knees, hips or ankles. Running, skipping or fast walking can help to tone the legs while swimming flexes the thighs and hips. But specific bending and stretching exercises for the feet and legs are the most effective of all.

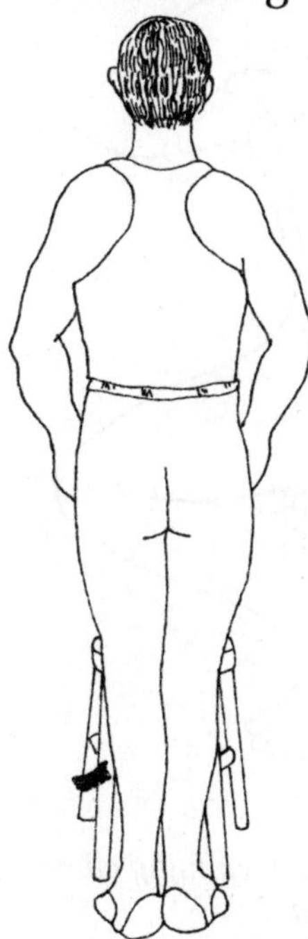

Knee bends

Dancers do pliés, or knee bends, to strengthen the legs, knees and ankles. Turn out the legs as much as possible from the hips, and pull in the buttocks to extend the leg muscles fully. You can gain extra stretch and strengthen the arches of the feet by taking your heels off the ground.

A1. *Face a bar or chair back and hold on with both hands. Place your feet in the first ballet position with the heels together, and the feet and legs turned out.*

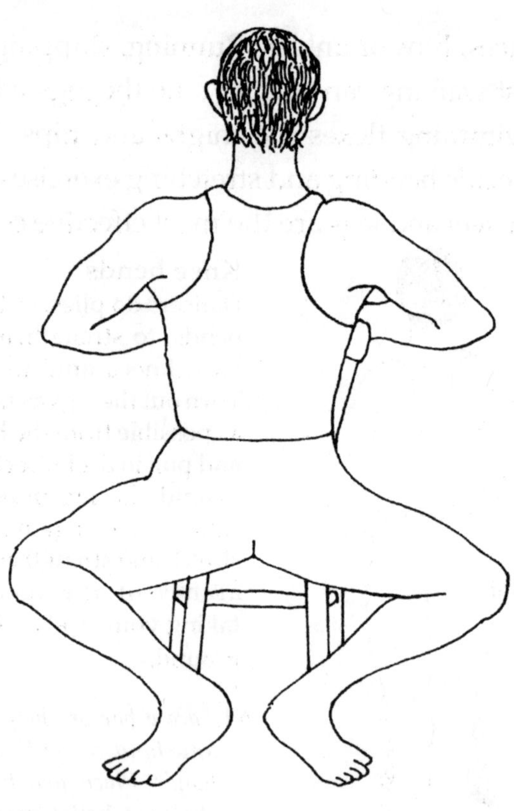

2. *Bend your knees, first half-way; then fully, allowing your heels to rise off the ground.*

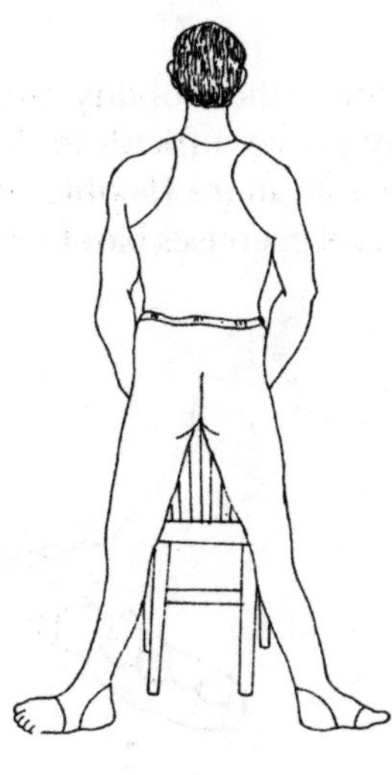

B1. *Take up the second ballet position, with your legs 2 ft. (60 cm) apart.*

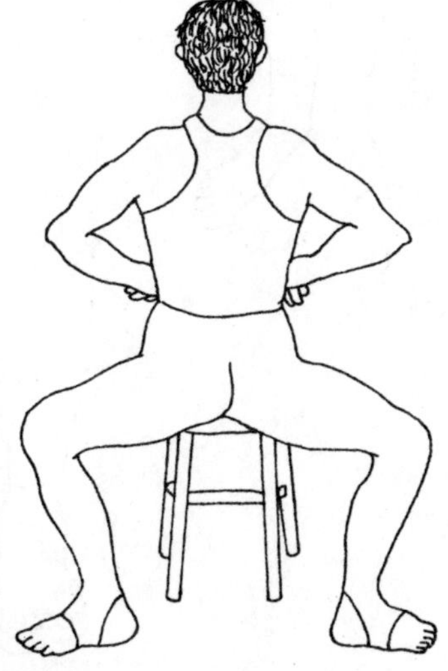

2. *Bend your knees, this time keeping your feet flat on the ground. Feel the stretch in your hips, groin and inner thigh.*

Ankles and feet

This exercise will help to improve the mobility and flexibility of your feet. It may prove difficult to do at first, but as your feet become more flexible, it should get easier. Always do foot exercises barefoot.

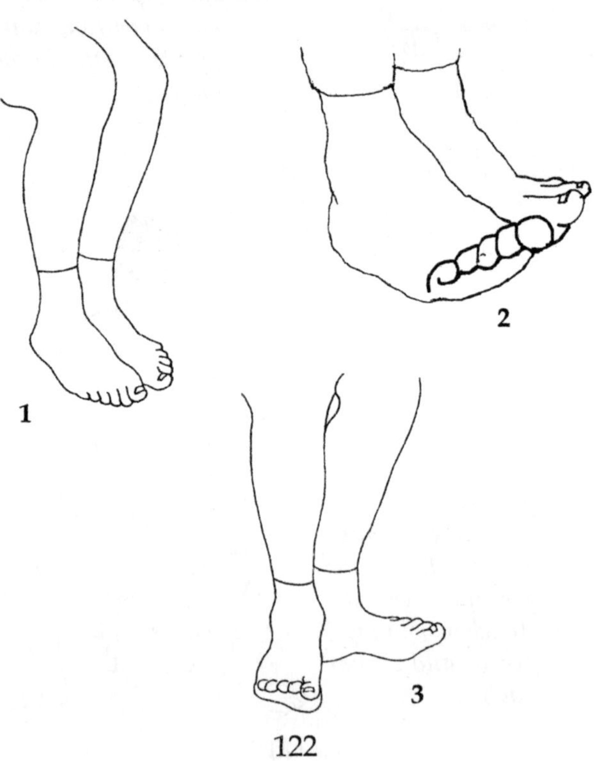

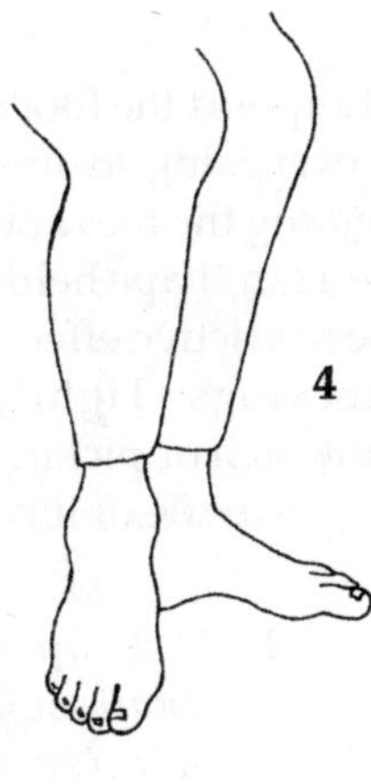

4

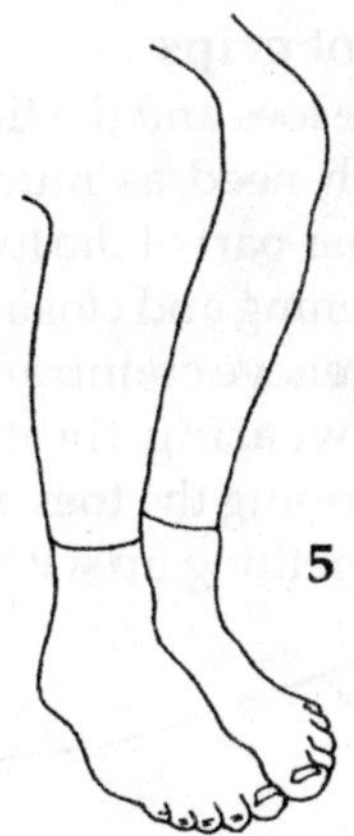

5

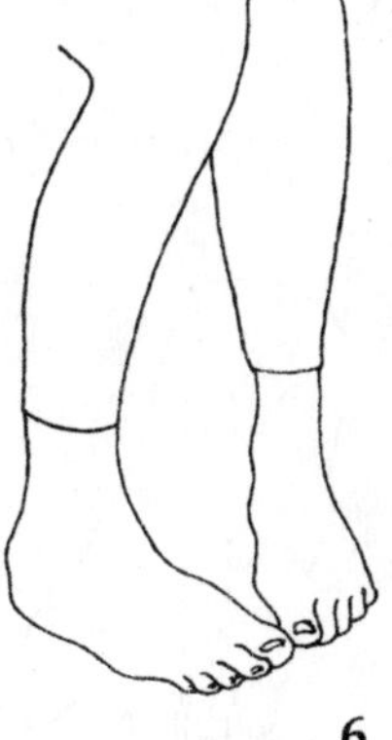

6

1. *Sit on a chair and place your feet together.*
2. *Raise them until only the heels rest on the ground.*
3. *Lift them out into an open position.*
4. *Lower your toes.*
5. *Slide your feet together.*
6. *Reverse the exercise, with your toes turned in and touching, and the weight on the balls of your feet. Slide your feet back to the starting position.*

Foot grips

The toes and the tiny muscles that support the foot's arch need as much flexing and exercising as any other part of the foot. Simply wriggling the toes and opening and closing them to make a fan shape helps to relieve cramp and overcome the restrictive effects of wearing tight shoes and stockings. Tightly gripping the toes and hollowing the arch or picking something up with the toes also improves flexibility.

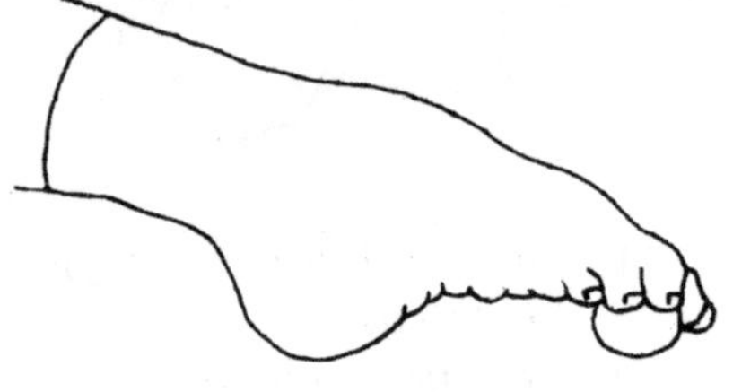

1. *Pick up a small soft ball (or a pencil) with your toes.*

1

2. *Open your toes to make a fan shape.*

2

Breathing

Oxygen is the basic stuff of life. Each cell of the body relies on it for fuel.

Most of the time we are not conscious of the fact that we are breathing, yet during a single day we take between 16,000 and 23,000 breaths. Each breath uses up about 250 mls of oxygen and disposes of about 200 mls of carbon dioxide. For us to feel relaxed and well, the balance of these two substances is the most important.

Under normal circumstances we cannot regulate the amount of oxygen in the air we breathe. But we can regulate the levels of oxygen and carbon dioxide within the body by changing the way we breathe.

Normally, our breathing is controlled by the parts of the brain that monitor the ratio of oxygen and carbon dioxide in the body—we exhale as soon as the level of carbon dioxide in the blood makes it more acid. Fast or very deep breathing (known as hyperventilation or over-breathing), causes the body to eliminate too much carbon dioxide. This may make the blood too alkaline, producing unpleasant side-effects such as dizziness, by cutting off supplies of carbon dioxide to the brain. Forced, unnatural styles and rhythms of breathing can, therefore, upset the finely tuned feedback mechanism that controls our oxygen intake and carbon dioxide output. Shallow, irregular breathing, which can be caused by illnesses involving the respiratory tract, faulty posture, or physical tension, also upsets the balance.

But you can control the way you breathe. In order to fill your lungs evenly with air, you need to breathe rhythmically from the diaphragm, the dome-like muscle between the chest and the abdominal cavity. This also pulls the air down into the lower lungs, where most of the blood circulates. There are several exercises that you can do to help you control your breathing and they are all based on diaphragmatic breathing. Some are dynamic, helping you to release tension, others have more of a tranquillizing effect. All are useful aids to relaxation.

Yoga and some forms of meditation also incorporate breathing techniques. In the long term, increasing the amount of exercise you take will also increase your lung capacity and help with the quality of your breathing.

Posture also influences the way we breathe. If you slouch, or your chest and rib-cage are slumped and concave, the diaphragm is immobilized and breathing is confined mainly to the upper chest area. Chest breathing puts strain on the heart as it must pump through more blood to carry the same amount of oxygen. It can also lead to increased blood pressure as the blood circulates more rapidly. Quick upper chest breathing generally produces cramped, shallow respiration which only fills about one quarter of the lung's capacity.

Whenever you are relaxing, try to regulate, quieten, or centre your breathing. You should do this especially when you are outdoors, whether walking or sitting in the garden or lying on a beach. Inhaling fresh, unpolluted air (especially by the sea, in the countryside, or at high altitudes), helps to refresh and clarify the mind and bring fresh supplies of oxygen-rich blood to all the tissues of your body.

Yoga

Yoga is a philosophy of living that had its genesis many thousands of years ago in India. It survives today throughout the world, as the oldest and most holistic system of mind-body fitness.

Literally translated, yoga means union, and it aims to unite physical, mental, and spiritual health. It induces spiritual awareness, deep relaxation, mental tranquillity, concentration and clarity, fused with physical strength and suppleness.

But in order to obtain this mind/body harmony and inner calm, it is not necessary to delve very deeply into the yogic philosophy—or to be a contortionist. You can take up yoga at any age and level of fitness. The postures (which are known as *asanas*) can be adapted to allow for physical injury or weakness. Go to a yoga class if you are unsure which positions to attempt. Unlike more vigorous exercise systems, the asanas are practised slowly, without pushing or jerking the body, so there is no risk of strain or injury.

Yoga is unique because it not only stretches all parts of the body, it also massages the internal organs and glands. And its coordinated system of breathing relaxes mind and body, stimulates the circulation and increases the supply of oxygen to all the tissues. The parts of the body which yoga stretches and tones most dramatically are the back, the stomach, the chest, and the lungs. The result is that the stiffening-up processes due to inactivity, tiredness, incorrect posture and ageing are reversed.

When practising yoga it is important to follow a sequence of asanas that has been structured carefully – you should not select one or two individual asanas and hope them to be beneficial. This is because the stretches of one position are balanced by counterstretches in the next. Do not skip on the relaxation periods that precede and follow each yoga session. Relaxation, of both body and mind is vital to yoga, making it a good way of banishing tension.

Meditation

Meditation works by emptying the conscious mind. You direct your thoughts away from yourself and your problems, far from your work, family, environment and relationships. As you do this, you begin gradually to transcend the everyday level of consciousness, the hurly-burly of the here and now, and open up pathways to those parts of the brain that deal with unconscious thought and experience.

When this happens, your arms or legs may begin to feel warm or heavy, and your head may begin to droop. In addition, your breathing will grow much shallower and slower as you become more and more relaxed and your mind will be divorced increasingly from your body and its immediate surroundings.

Meditation has been popular for over 5,000 years. Its chief appeal lies in its simplicity and in its undoubted benefits. It can quieten the surface-chatter of the brain, exorcising extraneous, intrusive, and stressful thoughts. And it has the additional advantage that you can practise it on your own, without professional guidance, wherever you can find a congenial, undisturbed space.

If you meditate regularly for about 20 minutes, once or twice a day, you can reduce your consumption of oxygen and production of carbondioxide by upto 20 per cent, lower your blood pressure, and reduce your level of blood lactate, a chemical produced in extra quantities at times of stress and anxiety.

Biofeedback monitoring shows that meditation encourages the brain to produce an evenly balanced pattern of alpha and theta brainwave rhythms, indicating that the body is relaxed and the mind calm, yet alert.

Regular meditation has helped people overcome addiction to tranquilizers and has reduced hypertension, insomnia, migraine, depression, anxiety, and other psychosomatic illnesses. It can also improve creativity, concentration, mental alertness, and memory, and stimulate physical energy.

Meditation relies on the close links between body and mind. When you meditate successfully, the alpha brain waves that are produced show that you have reached the most balanced, relaxed, and harmonious state your body is able to attain. This freedom from physical tension and mental strain allows the body to switch to the *relaxation response*, the complete opposite of the physical tension that occurs as a result of stress.

Recent research into the function of the human brain suggests that meditation expands brain function by encouraging a balance between the two separate hemispheres of the brain — the left-hand side, responsible for logical, reactional and scientific thought, and the (right-hand side) responsible for creative and imaginative work. The healthiest, the most productive and fulfilled people are usually those in whom the activity of these two hemispheres is well-balanced.

For the purposes of controlling and surviving stress and utilizing it creatively, concentrate on the therapeutic and relaxing benefits of meditation, rather than its deeper, more spiritual aspects. But whatever your attitude or goal in meditation, it will both improve your well-being and offer the added possibility of expanded creativity and enhanced sensory awareness.

Meditation Techniques

To meditate successfully you will need peace and quiet. Find a tranquil, comfortable environment where you can be alone and undisturbed for 20 to 30 minutes. Harsh lighting, a room that is too cold or too hot, noise and interruptions are all obstacles that can prevent you from achieving the level of physical and mental quietness that is necessary for meditation. Some people find that incense, dim lights, or soft, repetitive background music helps them to meditate. Others find environmental sounds like birds singing, rain falling or the sound of the ocean, helpful in creating the right mood. But you may prefer complete silence and as little sensory stimulation as possible.

Meditation, has two stages—physical relaxation, followed by focusing and emptying the mind. When you begin meditating, these initial stages may take time to attain.

Meditation and Breathing

Breathing forms a pivot between conscious, voluntary states of being and transcendent, involuntary states of relaxation. Concentrating on your breathing is an ideal mental focusing device which helps to block out other thoughts, blanking and quietening the mind by replacing mental clutter with a single object of contemplation.

When you are relaxed, close your eyes and begin to concentrate on the rhythm and feel of your breathing. This should be unforced and perhaps a little slower and shallower than usual. Imagine your stomach gently rising and falling with each in and out breath. For a while, think "in" as you breathe through your nose, and "out" as you breathe out through your nose or mouth. Then start to count each breath, either repeating "one", or counting from one to ten. Concentrate on each breath, allowing yourself to be totally hypnotized by it; exclude all other thoughts from your mind. If you are counting, visualize the numbers each time you exhale by mentally planting them in the centre of your stomach, Do not anticipate or rush the next number—let each one melt gently into the next.

Meditating on an Object

Instead of concentrating on your breathing, you may prefer to meditate by contemplating an object, for example, a single perfectly formed flower, a mandala or eastern symbolic design, or a flickering candle. Silently repeating to yourself a single sound or using a special audio tape are effective methods for many people.

Forward de-stressing

This is a very powerful way of overcoming fear. You create a very detailed and complete picture in your mind of yourself in the potentially stressful situation. Then you feel and experience, as fully as possible, everything that could go wrong. You follow this by feeling and experiencing everything you know you have in your power to prevent the problem being stressful. This *positive programming* is far better than simply willing yourself to do better.

Visualization

You may prefer a more visual approach to meditation. Imagining yourself in idyllic surroundings, watching the wide expanse of a blue ocean or walking through a sun-dappled forest, may evoke deep mental and physical relaxation. One of the most powerful benefits of this type of meditation is its power, when incorporating certain specific techniques, to counteract negative thinking, nervousness, anxiety, fear and low self-esteem.

Special imaging techniques help to balance the left-hand and right-hand hemispheres of the brain, sharpen memory, and improve sensory awareness. They can also control our so-called involuntary physical actions. These techniques are used extensively as a part of numerous anti-stress and self-improvement systems such as silva mind control and sophrology. They are increasingly being used by doctors, dentists, athletes, pilots, artists and teachers to defuse specifically stressful situations.

In particular, they can help overcome fear, apprehension and nervousness. Apprehension—fear before the event—can be very stressful; and the use of positive imagery can help us to replace our negative thoughts and face pain, challenge and difficult situations with new confidence. So positive imaging is increasingly used by psychologists as a part of the treatment for phobias and anxieties.

Using Visualization

Lie or sit down and relax your body, your breathing and your mind. Concentrate for a while on emptying your brain, focusing on the sound and rhythm of your breathing. Now imagine yourself lying or walking on a white, sandy beach. The sand is white and fine as talcum powder, tinged with pink. The sea is crystal clear, deep turquoise, or indigo blue, lapping at your feet. The breeze is gently caressing your body and hair. Feel the warm sun on your body, the sand between your toes, the sea spray on your face, and the water lapping over your legs and arms. Then imagine you are lying in the sea, floating. Feel the buoyancy of the deep blue or turquoise salty water support your body effortlessly as you float on your back, your face upturned towards the sun. Feel your body become warm and heavy as the sun's rays spread their gentle warmth all around.

You can extend this type of meditation by imagining yourself free of aches, pains, illness, infection and stress. See the part of your body that needs healing or strengthening becoming strong and perfectly formed. If you have an infection or inflammation, think of your white blood cells like fierce warriors or piranha fish attacking diseased unhealthy tissue and cells, destroying them and encouraging new healthy cells to multiply in their place. Imagine these warring cells carried along in the lymph fluids which sweep up the diseased unhealthy cells, along with poisonous wastes, and flush them out of your system forever. At the same time visualize fresh supplies of clean oxygen-rich blood, bathing and nourishing the healthy tissues and strengthening it. If you have migraine or tension headache or tight aching muscles, think of the muscles relaxing and lengthening; imagine your pulse rate and blood pressure lowering, swollen throbbing dilated blood vessels contracting and the pain diminishing.

Left-right Brain Exercises

This type of exercise strengthens and expands brain function by encouraging balance of the right-hand left-hand hemispheres of the brain. Practised regularly, it will help you to improve concentration and learning skills, to solve problems and to overcome nervousness, tension and stress.

Close your eyes and relax your body while breathing; empty your mind. Keep your eyes closed. Now concentrate on one side of your brain and one eye. Imagine with your right eye, and with the right side of your brain, that you see a tree in spring covered in pink and white blossoms. Now, using the left side of the brain, and the left eye, see the same tree draped in snow. Establish these two pictures clearly and distinctly and try and merge the images of the two trees into the centre of your brain where they become one tree covered in autumn foliage. You can devise further exercises based on the other senses, e.g. taste (eating a juicy apple and hot buttered toast), smell (smelling a rose and a pot of coffee), and sound (classical music and jazz), balancing and merging each on opposite sides of the brain in a similar way.

Massage and Acupressure

The relaxing, healing, and reviving powers of massage were recognized and recorded over 5,000 years ago. The therapeutic application of aromatic oils and unguents, and the practice of rubbing and pressing specific areas of the body to relieve pain and prevent illness, were common among the civilizations of ancient Egypt, India, China and Greece.

Today the time-honoured techniques of massage, together with allied skills such as reflexology and acupressure, are again popular. More recent types of western massage, such as Swedish massage, are also widely used to relax and tone the body.

The aim of any massage system, eastern or western, is to ease away muscular tension, to dispel tiredness and to reinforce depleted or unbalanced energy. Massage has the added benefit of helping you to prevent future physical weaknesses and strains. You can identify the prime tension spots, commonly found on the neck, shoulders and back, by laying your hand flat onto your partner's body. Tense muscles feel rock hard, like tight, knotted cords. You may also detect hard, fibrositic nodules of tissue. Relaxed muscles, on the other hand, feel rather like putty, firm but flexible.

The various stroking, rubbing, kneading, pulling, and hacking movements used in massage will help to relax these tight and tense muscles. They will also improve circulation and encourage the elimination of toxic waste.

Eastern pressure-point techniques follow the same principles as acupuncture. According to acupuncture the essential life force flows to all parts of the body through a system of meridians or energy lines. Acupressure and foot reflexology concentrate on balancing this flow of energy, by stimulating or sedating it. Pressure on the many acupuncture points all over the body can also strengthen or relax the internal organs, the spine, and the central nervous system. So these techniques are rather like acupuncture without needles using thumb and finger pressure to treat the various points. Back pain, menstrual cramp, headaches, sleeplessness, fatigue, depression and muscular tension, all respond well to this type of treatment. Acupressure can also be used as a self-help technique to relieve the discomfort associated with sinus disorders, migraine, neuralgia, and other stress-related problems.

Aromatherapy is a branch of massage that involves rubbing therapeutic plant essences into the body. Absorbing the oils via the skin and inhaling their scent, counteracts disharmony.

At their best, massage, acupressure and reflexology are sharing experiences in which the sense of touch is heightened. During massage you become more aware of the most subtle feelings of pleasure and discomfort. So trust and empathy between the person giving and the person receiving the massage, are essential if the receiver is to relax fully. The giver should warm his hands and flex them before beginning, and should never rush. The giver's movements should flow into each other imperceptibly, the hands remaining in perpetual contact with the receiver's body.

Personal Space and Comfort

Our environment is an extension of ourselves. We adapt our immediate surroundings to suit our individual needs and comforts, so that our homes offer us the opportunity to be truly ourselves. Fashioning our environment according to preferences of colour, style and dimensions, is a method of self-expression, a personal statement directly related to our sense of identity and a reflection of our emotional security and sense of belonging. Since environment and mood are closely linked, our surroundings, if they are to be truly relaxing and nurturing, should be as stress-free as possible. The ideal stress-proofed home is one that shows a balanced choice of personal style and mood, sound and stillness, and a harmonious synthesis of different colours, light and shade.

The quality and comfort of any home can be undermined in various ways. Some of the causes are easy to recognize and to deal with. Removing unpleasant smells, controlling extremes of temperature and coping with dirt and untidiness are part of the everyday business of running a home. To do this efficiently, carry out all your housekeeping work routinely and methodically on a rota basis, making sure you store and return things to their proper place so that you know where to find them.

Clutter and disorganization can create mental stress, and lead to worry, anger and wastage of time when you search for lost and misplaced possessions. Tidying up as you go along (for example, during cooking or when changing your clothes) prevents clutter from building up, in the first place. If you are untidy, clear up at least two or three times a week.

Broad or environmental stresses, such as noise and bad light, can be more insidious and less easy to control. Noise is a subtle stress factor and its effect is cumulative. It can lead to loss of concentration, irritability and insomnia. It can also cause headaches and muscular tension. If noise is a problem, start by reducing the levels that you can control yourself. To cut out external noise, try wax earplugs. Double glazing is an effective way of cutting out street noise.

Light is another influence over how relaxed we are. Most of us feel happier, healthier and more energetic in bright, sunny weather. When we are constantly surrounded by artificial light, we tend to feel tired and depressed. This is not simply a psychological effect. Scientists have recently discovered a link between natural daylight and hormone levels, emotional well-being and reproductivity. Installing specially designed lights that mimic natural full-spectrum light can help to reduce seasonal depression and to improve concentration and energy.

There are many other ways of shaping your environment. Use time, ingenuity and above all imagination to create areas of private space, and adapt your home to your body's needs and habits. Trust your instincts in choosing colour schemes, background fragrances, houseplants and music. These are a few ways in which you can style, enrich and stress-proof your personal surroundings.

Tips for Stress Reduction

Life's myriad changes often lead to an accumulation of stress. Here is a compendium of simple, common-sense strategies for transforming mental and physical tension into energy creatively and effectively expressed. None of these strategies are new. Many will be familiar to you but we often need to be reminded. Circle the ones you would like to remember more often. Then add your own to the list.

- Take time to be alone on a regular basis, to listen to your heart, check your intentions, re-evaluate your goals and your activities.
- Simplify your life! Start eliminating the trivia.

- Take deep, slow breaths frequently, especially while on the phone, in the car, or waiting for something or someone. Use any opportunity to relax and revitalize yourself.
- Plan to do something each day that brings you joy, something that you love to do, something just for you.
- When you are concerned about something, talk it over with someone you trust, or write down your feelings.
- Say "No" when asked to do something you really do not want to do. Read a book on assertiveness if you have trouble doing this in a firm but kind way.
- Remember to use helpful clichés such as, "In a hundred years, who will know the difference?" "What doesn't weaken

us, makes us stronger," or "Whether you think you can or you think you can't, you're right."

- Exercise regularly!
- Remember, it takes less energy to get an unpleasant task done "right now" than to worry about it all day.
- Take time to be with nature, people, music and children. Even in the city, noticing the seasonal changes of the sky or watching people's faces can be a good harmonizer.
- Practise consciously doing one thing at a time, keeping your mind focused on the present. Do whatever you are doing more slowly, more intentionally, and with more awareness and respect.

- Choose not to waste your precious present life on guilt about the past, or concern for the future.
- Learn a variety of relaxation techniques and practise at least one regularly.
- Let your eyes be soft and relaxed.
- When you find yourself repeatedly angry in similar situations, ask yourself, "What can I learn from this?" Anyone or anything that can make you angry is showing you how you let yourself be controlled by expectations of how someone or something should be. When we accept others, ourselves and situations for what they are, we become more effective in influencing them to change in the way that we would like them to.

- Become more aware of the demands you place on yourself, your environment, and on others to be different from how they are at any moment. Demands are tremendous sources of stress.
- If your schedule is busy, prioritize your activities and do the most important ones first.
- When you read your mail, act on it immediately, do not put it off.
- Take frequent relaxation breaks.
- Organize your life to include time for fun, spontaneity, and open spaces. Set a realistic schedule allowing some transition time between activities. Eliminate unnecessary commitments.
- Smile and laugh more.
- Learn to delegate responsibility.

- Treat yourself to a massage, or learn to massage your own neck, shoulders and feet.
- Monitor your intake of sugar, salt, caffeine and alcohol.
- Create and maintain a personal support system – people with whom you can be "vulnerable."
- Seek out friends or professional help when you feel unable to cope.
- Be more kind to yourself and others.
- Appreciate the flow of change moment to moment. Welcome change as an opportunity and challenge to learn and grow.
- Watch clouds or waves on water. Listen to music or the sounds around you. Notice the silence between sounds and the space between objects and thoughts.

- When you notice you are stressed, smile tenderly to yourself, and breathe and let flow — Ahhh…
- Use your own distress to teach yourself to be more patient, caring, and compassionate towards yourself and others.
- Remember to stop and smell the flowers!